WHAT IF LIFE CAME WITH A USER GUIDE?

WHAT IF LIFE CAME WITH A USER GUIDE?

How to overcome negative self-talk,
deal with difficult people
and adjust to challenging situations

Deanne Duncombe

ISBN: 978-0-6455720-0-1 (paperback)
ISBN: 978-0-6455720-1-8 (ebook)

A catalogue record for this
book is available from the
National Library of Australia

Cover image by Ekaterina Chvileva – dreamstime.com
Edited by Phaedra Pym – awaywithwords.net.au
Book design and production by Eric and Thymen Hoek – exlibris.com.au
Author photograph by Olive and Maeve - oliveandmaeve.com

Permissions

Introduction—The Iceberg Way of Being diagram is based on a similar diagram created by Carole Lewis and is used with permission from Carole Lewis https://carolelewis.hk

Chapter 1—The Moods table is adapted from Sieler (2007) and is used with permission from Alan Sieler.

Chapter 4—Direct quote from Sieler (2003) describing Way of Being used with permission from Alan Sieler.

Chapter 5—Direct quote from Sieler (2003) describing anxiety used with permission from Alan Sieler.

Chapter 8—Grounding process adapted from Sieler (2003) and used with permission from Alan Sieler.

Chapter 10—The extract from 'A manager's guide to difficult conversations in the workplace'. *Fair Work Australia.* (Accessed 4 June, 2023). https://www.fairwork.gov.au/sites/default/files/migration/712/managers-guide-to-difficult-conversations-in-the-workplace.pdf, found on https://www.fairwork.gov.au, is used in accordance with the copyright statement https://www.fairwork.gov.au/website-information/copyright under Creative Commons 3.0 License from Creative Commons Australia, https://creativecommons.org/licenses/by/3.0/au/legalcode

Disclaimer

The material in this publication is of the nature of general comment only and does not represent professional advice. It is not intended to provide specific guidance for individual circumstances, and it should not be relied on as the basis for any decision to take action or not take action on any matter which it covers. Readers should obtain professional advice where appropriate before making any such decision. To the maximum extent permitted by law, the author and publisher disclaim all responsibility and liability to any person, arising directly or indirectly from any person taking or not taking action based on the information in this publication.

The coaching conversations in this book are a work of fiction. Unless otherwise stated, the names, characters, businesses, places, events, and incidents used in the coaching conversations are either the product of the author's imagination or used in a fictitious manner. Any resemblance to actual events or actual persons, living or dead, is purely coincidental unless the author indicates they are talking about actual persons or events.

Acknowledgement of Country

I acknowledge the Ngunnawal people as the traditional custodians of the land on which I live, work and wrote this book, and pay respect to Elders past, present and emerging. I further acknowledge and respect all Aboriginal and Torres Strait Islander people of Australia and their continuing connection to Country, culture, and community.

Dedication

To Rob, Erin and Alice. Thank you for always being there to support me in following my dreams. With all my love, always.

Acknowledgements

This book's journey started years ago when I was feeling over-whelmed, incompetent and out of my depth. While I was not consciously aware of it at the time, I declared that things would change. I also asked for help. That was a huge turning point in my life. I offer the deepest appreciation and gratitude to Ian Higginbottom for his patient coaching during that time. Ian helped me get out of my own way when I couldn't do it alone. Without a doubt, this book and much of who I am today would not exist without Ian's stellar efforts in helping me to see life differently.

Alan Sieler is a world leader in Ontological Coaching. He is also someone who has supported me greatly and whose work I very much respect and admire. I will always be grateful to have been one of Alan's students. As I have paved my own path in the Ontological Coaching world, I have appreciated Alan's support and guidance. I thank Alan for his generosity in reviewing my manuscript and writing the foreword. To have my work reviewed and commented on by one of the best in the Ontological Coaching world is an honour and a privilege. I am in gratitude.

Dan Newby's interpretation of emotions is superb. I admire his work profoundly and consider it a huge gift to the world. To have Dan give his time so generously to review and offer feedback on my manuscript was an honour. I offer my deepest appreciation, thanks, and gratitude to Dan for the privilege of his amazing support and encouragement and for the beautiful gift that is his interpretation of emotions.

The love of my family is something for which I am incredibly grateful. To my husband and daughters, thank you for being there with me in life and during the creation of this book. I may have written the words, but your support, encouragement and sacrifices helped to create it. To my mum, late dad, and my siblings and their families, thank you for loving me, encouraging me and believing in me.

Huge thanks to Kate McHenry and Leonie Townsend for being my cheer squad. They read nearly every version of my manuscript, provided feedback, laughed with me at the challenging parts, cheered me on at the good bits, and gave me the occasional kick in the pants when I needed it. These two incredibly giving women offered an amazing level of support. Love and gratitude for their efforts, which I have no doubt are a huge reason this book exists.

A dedicated group of readers is a gift. Thank you to the beta readers who kept my manuscript on track, suggested edits and gave me guidance and support when I needed it. I offer immense appreciation to a_adams89 (from Fiverr.com), Lana Stacey, Idot Wong, Jeremy Stunt, Yoga Nesadurai, Carole Lewis and Chris Chittenden. Their gift of feedback helped me see what my book could become.

One of the biggest lessons I have learnt in writing this book is to never underestimate the power of an awesome production team. Firstly, I offer an absolute tonne of gratitude to Phaedra Pym from A Way with Words for her amazing editing. Phaedra made editing so much fun while also showing me how to put myself in the shoes of my readers – she has my heartfelt gratitude. It is a journey I have loved, and I value Phaedra's considerable efforts. Eric and Thymen Hoek from Exlibris were the calm, patient responders to my many questions and I feel incredibly blessed to have had them on my team. Their cover design, book design, proofreading and practical advice have made an incredible difference, and I am both delighted and grateful for their support.

Contents

WHAT IF LIFE CAME WITH A USER GUIDE?

List of Figures

List of Tables

Foreword

It is a great pleasure to introduce Deanne's delightfully titled book. I regard this well-written book to be a very useful guide on how to cultivate living from a self-authoring mode of consciousness. What I find particularly appealing about this book is how the chapters are structured around important existential questions, some of which you may have been well aware of, others that you may have had peripheral awareness of, and others that you had not even considered.

I consider Deanne's offering to be a valuable contribution to addressing two fundamental existential questions, which are:

- How am I to live?
- How can I live well?

In what seems like an increasingly volatile and uncertain world, these are questions that go to the heart of the quality of our existence. They are significant questions that are an integral part of being human, and although they may not be at the forefront of our thoughts and in our immediate awareness, they are nevertheless constantly present. The role of questions in the quality of our lives is worth expanding upon and will be returned to in the closing section of this foreword.

Being 'thrown' into the world

When we emerged from the womb and eventually began to literally find our feet in life, nobody provided us with a handy guide on how to engage with and participate in life. Philosopher Martin Heidegger wrote that we are 'thrown' into the world – not literally, of course – that we randomly find ourselves in the world, having no say in the family, society and historical life circumstances into which we were born and grew up.

As biological entities, we constantly seek to adapt to the environments in which we find ourselves, which are not only physical environments but also environments of meaning that consist of emotions, moods, language, conversations, customs and social practices. Our parents and other elders most likely tried to provide us with some sort of structure for how to live, which included taking responsibility for aspects of our physiology, what is appropriate to say in different situations, and how to conduct ourselves emotionally in different settings. We also experienced informal learning from our peers – in play and conversations.

From this multitude of experiences, we absorbed a wide range of learning and 'life lessons' that formed our interpretations about how to live and function adequately in different settings. Another philosopher, Edmund Husserl, wrote that we all live in a 'life-world', which is all the immediate experiences, activities and contacts that make up our individual world. For Husserl, 'the ground of all knowledge is lived experience'.

As unique individuals, we did not all form the same meaning of life and how to live, continually creating interpretations that made sense to us at the time. Every decision we have made and how we have behaved has been our interpretation of how to live well in the circumstances that confronted us. Our learning from past experiences has provided an important orientation for the future, informing us how to engage with others, as well as make sense of and participate in the many different situations we will encounter.

Not having a blueprint for how we can live well means that we create life as we go, making it up 'on the run', and finding ways to navigate in a world that can, at times, be experienced as confusing and complex.

The challenge of developing a self-authoring mode of existence

Learning to live well can be thought of as a never-ending process of complex skill acquisition, with many life skills involving subtle learning, such as the appropriate distance to stand from someone in a conversation, how to compose an email or a text message to a particular person in a specific situation, or how to be socially appropriate in taking turns to speak in a conversation.

What is interesting is that learning a myriad of skills for how to live well is largely left to chance. As this book's title indicates, there is no user guide to help us navigate the often puzzling and sometimes frustrating maze of life. While we can absorb important learning from our parents, teachers, other elders, and peers, we are not provided with a specific curriculum to guide us in the acquisition of appropriate life skills, let alone direct personal support and guidance to enable us to enact such skills.

Our developmental task as we grew up was to make appropriate meaning and develop the requisite skills for living well. In his book, *In Over Our Heads: The Mental Demands of Modern Life*, Robert Kegan wrote that life is like a curriculum that places demands on us to respond successfully if we are to live well. He made a very important distinction between two fundamentally different levels or orders of adult consciousness that shape how we observe and navigate daily life. Levels of consciousness can be thought of as fundamental existential spaces that we live from that inform us how to perceive and act in the world.

Kegan called one of these levels of consciousness the 'socialised mind'. This is a mode of observing and operating in the world in which we have successfully learned how to be responsible citizens who do not require supervision. In other words, we can participate in the various social practices and manners of engaging with each other that are acceptable. We have all been through a lengthy process, from early childhood to becoming an adult, to develop this level of consciousness.

However, Kegan's thesis is that the socialised existential space is no longer sufficient for living well in our complex, rapidly changing pluralistic societies. He advocates the development of another level of consciousness for the wellbeing of individuals and society. He calls this level of consciousness the 'self-authoring mind'. In this fundamental existential space, the requirements for being a responsible adult have been absorbed. However, the individual seeks to constructively critique some of the 'lessons of life' they have unquestioningly been living from in a socialised mind. We no longer unthinkingly act from what Kegan calls the 'scripts' of life that we learned as we grew up, which authored our life. In this different existential space, we constructively critique the scripts and rewrite some of them to become more self-authoring. This does not mean that we become anarchists or live from an 'anything goes, I'm an individual' mentality. We still remain responsible citizens but begin to find greater agency in how we can live without being trapped in the myriad of 'have to's' and 'should's' that accompany the socialised mind and enter into an existential space of having a broader perspective of life that contains more possibility and choice.

While Deanne refers to this book as a user guide, it is not a technical manual with specific steps to follow to successfully manage some life issue. Each chapter is an invitation to consider an important theme that relates to everyday life and offers a range of perspectives and skills that have been derived from the discipline of Ontological Coaching. Overall, this book is about how to engage with life from an ontological perspective.

Ontological Coaching uses the expression 'Way of Being' to understand the perceptual and behavioural patterns that we have learned to live from, many of which have become ingrained, taken for granted and out-of-awareness. An ontological approach to coaching offers a way of identifying and changing unhelpful patterns by making shifts in our Way of Being. Each of the chapters in this book provides an opportunity to make beneficial shifts in your Way of Being.

Part of the beauty of the ontological approach to better under-standing ourselves and improving our life is that we don't need to rely on a coach all the time. The coach can get us started, but once we learn key concepts and develop new skills, we can engage in what is called 'generative learning'. This means that when we learn about important aspects of our Way of Being, we can continually self-generate change in our Way of Being.

Questions and thinking

Let us now bring the focus back to the importance of questions, including existential questions. One of the publications of the previously mentioned philosopher Martin Heidegger is a book titled *What Is Called Thinking?* For some readers, Heidegger's perspective on what constituted thinking was somewhat controversial. He contended that thinking is not having thoughts. Indeed, he claimed that most of the time most of us don't think. Heidegger's perspective is that genuine thinking involves the asking of unusual questions, which have the potential to stimulate novel thoughts and new paths of thinking.

For Heidegger, thinking is being thought-provoking. He urged us to inquire into those matters that normally remain unquestioned concerning our everyday existence and traditions. The word 'provoke' comes from the Latin word 'provocare', with 'vocare' meaning 'to call'. According to Heidegger, that which is thought-provoking calls to us, inviting a response. That which is *most* thought-provoking calls us in the sense of calling-to-action; it calls us and invites us to engage in the possibility of taking different action to bring about a different outcome.

Thought-provoking questions can sometimes be considered as being unsettling, even upsetting at times. However, the potential power of questions is that they orient us to a different perspective, which has the potential to open up a different world of possibility and action. Some potentially thought-provoking existential questions are:

- What questions are you 'living in' about the quality of your life and who and how you are as a person? The expression 'living in' means that which dwells within you that you are aware of and not aware of.
- What questions are you not asking regarding how you live and how you can live well?

One of the risks of engaging with questions is that we can immediately seek an answer or a solution. However, existential questions do not always readily lend themselves to nicely packaged answers. A crucial part of thinking is being prepared to 'stay with the question' or 'live with the question'. In other words, let the question sit and percolate in the background and be patient and open to an answer arising or 'bubbling to the surface'.

I consider that Deanne has created a book for thinkers in the Heidegger mode of thinking. Reading and reflecting on the chapters may open up other existential questions for you. I believe there is much potential value in not only reading each chapter carefully but also in returning to specific chapters when you are confronted with challenging circumstances.

Alan Sieler

Director, Ontological Coaching Institute

Author of Volumes I, II, III and IV of
Coaching to the Human Soul: Ontological Coaching and Deep Change

Preface

'The problem we are trying to fix is that you are useless!'

In one sentence, my manager turned my biggest fear into a reality. He viewed me as a failure. My insides collapsed. I didn't know how to react. Everything I had ever learnt about life involved being nice to others. How should I respond to a manager who refused to play nicely because he saw me as a failure? I took a deep breath. From somewhere within, I pretended not to be hurt. I held back my tears, indignation and fear of failure. My boss remained unaware of the impact of his words.

I focused on my job, afraid of the flow-on effect of any show of emotion. However, on the inside, I was frustrated and disappointed. By not speaking up, I had allowed my power to be taken from me. Again.

Later, once I was alone, I cried. Would I ever again experience a working environment where people trusted and valued me?

I saw myself as a good person. Yet, my over-inflated need to follow the rules and 'do the right thing' often created a struggle for me. When faced with uncertainty about how to do the right thing, I would struggle more, and anxiety would set in. I don't mean a diagnosed anxiety disorder. Instead, I felt anxious about the consequences of doing the wrong thing. I lived in fear of failure. The more I tried to avoid failure, the more it seemed to find me. Often, I seemed to be creating the very thing I was trying to avoid.

Most of us are trying to do our best. From our experience of interacting with life, we create rules for living. Our rules become a part of us, infused in our language, moods and emotions, and housed in our body. We are often unaware that our rules exist, let alone what they are creating for us. Because we are unaware of our rules and their effect on our existence, we don't always get the outcomes we are chasing. This is because our lack of awareness removes the possibility of choice. Without choice, we limit our flexibility and resilience. Our actions lead us, rather than us leading our actions.

My work situation, although a challenging time, became an enriching life experience. It began a journey of discovery that led me to better understand myself and others around me. I sought help and I learnt how to make deliberate choices about my interactions with others. I learnt to shift some of my rules for behaving in life to bring about outcomes that served me. I started by noticing the questions behind the choices I make in life:

- What stories, moods and emotions underpin my behaviours?
- Why do these stories, moods and emotions exist?
- How are my stories, moods and emotions sitting in my body?
- What sensations are my stories, moods and emotions causing in my body?

By becoming curious about the stories, moods and emotions, and bodily sensations behind my choices and actions, I could understand my actions and behaviours. So how does this apply to everyday life?

Have you ever been standing in a queue when someone has pushed in front of you? What did you say to yourself and others? What moods or emotions did you experience? What sensations did you notice in your body? Now reflect on how you reacted. How did your reaction relate to the stories, moods and emotions, and feelings in your body? We aren't born with stories, moods and emotions, and bodily sensations attached to social situations, so what past learning generated these for you? With this new awareness, what would you change if someone were to push in front of you again? Perhaps you wouldn't change anything. That's fine. You have already enabled choice in the action you will take next by noticing what was behind your actions. Deliberate choice leads us to more useful outcomes.

Before becoming curious about the source of my behaviours, I suffered. I doubted myself. I lived in fear and anxiety. Making decisions challenged me because I didn't trust myself when faced with uncertainty. I would not allow myself to have a voice. I always put other people first, even if the sacrifice of doing so meant my suffering increased. When I put aside my self-judgement and drew my attention to my language, moods and emotions, and body, I shifted the way I interacted with life. I became a leader of my life, choosing the direction of my path. Instead of becoming defined by the labels my bullying manager gave me, I found my power and chose how to respond to the hurt. Awareness gives us choice, and choice gives us flexibility, resilience and self-leadership.

In writing this book, I want to help you shift some of the suffering that comes with the challenges of interacting in everyday life. I hope the ideas in this book help you respond from a place of resourcefulness, choosing the actions you would like to take to achieve the outcomes you are striving for. I want to give you the possibility of navigating the challenges of everyday life in a way that is useful for you.

Introduction

Language is used to listen, create stories, state opinions and facts, coordinate action and make sense of our world. Moods and emotions help move us to act based on how we are interpreting the world in each moment. Our language, moods and emotions live in our body. This is evident when we observe how our breathing, physical sensations, comfort and posture shift as our language, moods and emotions change.

The combination of our language, moods and emotions, and body is known as our Way of Being. Our Way of Being generates our actions and behaviours, including how we observe ourselves and others in the world, the choices we make, the things we do, how we behave and the outcomes we create. Different ways of being generate different actions and behaviours. This means an action or behaviour may be available to us from one Way of Being but not from another.

We are often unaware of what is happening in our Way of Being because we don't know how to observe it. However, our Way of Being offers valuable learning as we navigate everyday life. This is because our Way of Being sits behind every action. When our actions are not serving us, our Way of Being is the source of many clues.

To demonstrate how our Way of Being influences our actions, consider the following scenario. Imagine it is dark and your hear a loud noise outside.

- What actions would you take from a scared Way of Being? What would you be saying to yourself? How would your body feel?
- What actions would you take from an angry Way of Being?

- What if you told yourself the neighbourhood possum caused the noise on its nightly visit? How would you react in that case?
- How would you react if your shoulders were dropped and you had a closed torso and concave spine (known as a 'diminished body')?

I suspect you could identify the actions you would take based on each underlying Way of Being listed.

Before going any further, let's consider why it is important for us to understand our Way of Being if we want to bring about different outcomes in our interactions with others.

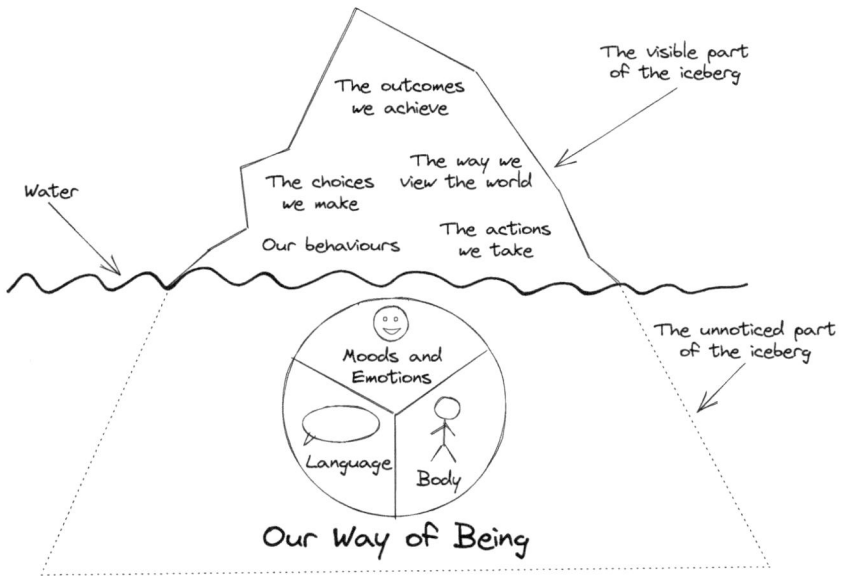

Figure 1: *Our Way of Being underpins our actions, behaviours, choices and outcomes*[1]

Figure 1 shows how our Way of Being underpins the things we do. While these 'things we do' may be visible, our Way of Being is often invisible to us, much like the submerged part of an iceberg.

---

1 Adapted with permission from Carole Lewis' interpretation of the Way of Being model https://carolelewis.hk

We aren't always aware of what is happening beneath the surface (within our Way of Being) or how and why it influences our actions. However, it is always within us: our language, moods and emotions, and body impact what we do in every moment of life.

If we aren't aware of what lies beneath the surface of an iceberg, it is difficult to choose the most useful actions for navigating the iceberg. In the same way, if we are unaware of the Way of Being beneath the surface of our actions, we are less selective of our actions for navigating life. Instead, we take action based on our Way of Being without realising why. And when our actions don't serve us, they can lead to suffering.

Our Way of Being is the source of our actions and behaviours. As the source, it makes sense that shifting our actions and behaviours means first shifting our Way of Being. To shift the visible (actions and behaviours), we must start by understanding and shifting the invisible (our Way of Being).

As we navigate life, we can easily fall into the trap of assuming that life is what it is and we can't change it. This fixed mindset leaves us powerless to change and create the life we want to lead. Understanding and shifting our Way of Being allows us to be resourceful in our approach to life, making it possible to generate new actions and create the future we want through deliberate choice.

This book offers ideas and questions that support us in navigating everyday life. We discover these ideas and the questions to ask through the life of Maggie, a fictional character who is struggling at work. She engages a coach, Alex, to support her. Each chapter shares a new step in Maggie's journey and offers a new set of questions to ask.

Although Maggie has a coach, this does not mean the ideas shared in this book are only successful for those who engage a coach. Instead, the coaching conversations demonstrate how to apply the ideas in this book to everyday life. These same ideas can be applied using personal reflection without a coach.

Each chapter links to our Way of Being. The first four chapters focus on how Maggie changed her path and asked for help. These chapters also delve more deeply into the concept of our Way of Being and what it means to use your Way of Being as a source of learning and exploration to fulfil the new actions you wish to create.

In Chapters 5 to 10, Maggie and Alex explore worry, anxiety, doubt, emotions, dealing with difficult people, learning to speak up and having difficult conversations.

While many of Maggie's challenges involve work, the ideas are relevant in any part of our lives, including relationships and family dynamics. Furthermore, the ideas adopted by Maggie and Alex can be mixed and matched to apply to your situation in whatever way works for you.

Chapter 11 explores a six-step model for navigating life. The model summarises the approach used by Alex and Maggie and is provided to support you in your own personal reflection as you navigate life.

Most chapters in this book comprise four sections:

- *The Story* contains the fictional coaching conversation between Maggie and Alex.
- *The Learning* provides detail and theory to complement and extend the coaching conversation.
- *A Deeper Reflection* provides some questions and activities to enable a deeper personal reflection using the distinctions and ideas presented in the chapter.
- *Key Points* summarises the main takeaways from the chapter.

The ideas in this book are based on an ontological approach, focusing on our Way of Being in life. Using this approach enables us to set aside our judgements about who we are, using curiosity to see our Way of Being as a source of learning.

There is no right or wrong in this paradigm. If your Way of Being is not serving you well, that doesn't make it wrong, nor does it make you a failure. We are all legitimate human beings, taking legitimate action from a legitimate Way of Being. The question is not whether we are right or wrong but whether our being and doing serve us as we navigate the challenges of everyday life.

As you read this book, I hope you discover new ways of seeing and understanding your Way of Being – the less obvious qualities beneath the surface – and ways to take action and apply the lessons learnt to shift your Way of Being and, in so doing, create a future that serves you.

CHAPTER 1

What should I do when life isn't going as I want it to?

The Story

So far, Maggie wouldn't call the year a highlight.

I made a mistake in taking this job. The job I am doing is not the job my manager offered me. I am clearly not the right fit. If only I had known before agreeing to take it on.

Maggie had changed jobs because life had changed her plan. One minute, everything seemed perfect. The next, her father died and she became unwell. She took time off work. Her boss at the time had saved several urgent tasks for her return. However, ongoing grief and illness had left Maggie struggling. Her boss showed no compassion.

Do your job. Your private life isn't your work life. Just deliver.

Yes, Maggie didn't plan to change jobs, but she wanted to escape her boss and his lack of compassion. So she'd taken the first job offered. That's how Maggie had ended up an emotional wreck, feeling like a failure and hating today.

I am not good enough. No one else ever struggles. Everyone around me is competent. I am getting things so wrong. I want to do the right thing, but I can't.

The tears on Maggie's lips were salty.

Crying again. It's all I seem to do. Stupid job!

The ringing phone interrupted Maggie's thoughts.

Oh, great. Olivia is calling me. Not now. I can't talk now. I need time.

Maggie and Olivia met a month ago when Maggie started her new job. They became friends almost the minute they met in the staff kitchen. For now, though, Maggie wouldn't answer the phone. She couldn't. The phone rang out.

Why do I struggle? Why am I not enough? My stupid confidence is always letting me down. Why? I mean, I am not a complete failure. Some things I do well. I enjoy my life. My friends care about me. Most people say I work hard. Some people even say I am capable. Why can't I be confident? Something always stops me from grabbing onto life and charging forward. I don't want to be afraid of taking risks.

Maggie lifted her glasses from her face, wiping the tears with a tissue before putting her glasses back in place.

I can't keep going like this. I will break. Plus, others can tell I am a wreck. My self-confidence has always been low, but at least I used to be competent at work. How do I become competent again? Why can't I do that?

Maggie's tears fogged up her glasses, rendering them useless. She removed them.

This job is too much. I need to understand all the details, but my current project is huge. I can't understand everything. I'll never be comfortable in this job. Knowing everything is impossible.

The disintegrated tissue in Maggie's hand no longer did its job. Maggie grabbed another from the box.

I want to leave this job, but I can't. I will look like a failure. What would people say?

Maggie felt her phone vibrate before the ringtone sounded.

Oh great, it's Olivia again. She's not giving up. I guess I'll have to talk to her, even if I'm not ready.

'Hello.'

'Thank goodness you've answered!'

'Why?'

'Because I'm worried about you!'

'Oh. Well, I am fine.'

I am so not fine!

'I don't believe you. You seemed unhappy this morning, and then you disappeared. What's going on?'

'You missed the part where I am the new incompetent manager working in the job from hell.'

'I agree; I wouldn't want your job. But you are *not* incompetent.'

'Tell that to the senior managers pushing me into a corner and the twenty staff expecting direction.'

A pause.

'Maggie?'

'Yes?'

'Talk to me. What's the problem?'

'Olivia, I can't do this job. I should have stayed at my last job. Why didn't I ask my previous manager to spread out my deadlines and help me? Instead, I got angry and jumped ship. Now, here I am, Princess Failure, in a job I'm not fit for.'

'You're being too hard on yourself, Maggie. Your father died, you became unwell, and your boss wasn't supportive. He didn't understand your suffering. Don't blame yourself.'

'I need to take responsibility.'

'Sure, take responsibility, but don't blame yourself. What happened in your last job is not your fault, and neither is what's happening in this job. Perhaps life is trying to teach you something.'

'Well, whatever it is, I hope I can learn it soon because this current situation is getting old.'

'How can I help?'

Five seconds of silence dragged on to become an awkward ten.

Maggie sighed. 'I'm out of my depth. How do I even do this job?

I am too uncertain about the environment to decide anything. It's like I'm on a wild ride travelling at breakneck speed. I am oblivious to where we are, and we're travelling so fast the street signs are a blur. Yet, I am responsible for the direction. In most other jobs, I planned my way toward success. This job is too big for me. I signed up for a job with no staff, and now I'm managing twenty. There's no way I would have accepted the role if they'd told me that. I did not plan on being a manager.'

'Well, the current situation is where you're at. And I understand things are crazy. To be honest, this place *is* crazy. So, what's the plan?'

'I want to leave.'

'Well, leave.'

'The problem is, I need the money. Plus, I don't want a four-week employment term on my resume. A short time in a job shouts "failure".'

'What else can you do?'

'Stay until a decent job comes up, and hope no one fires me in the meantime.'

'Is that your only plan?'

'Well, what else is there? How do I change a horrible situation that I can't control?'

'What about asking for help?'

'How can anyone help me if the situation is beyond my control? I can't change anything.'

'Well, you can change your perspective and apply new strategies.'

You don't understand. I can't do this.

'Where can I get help from? You're the only person I trust at work, and everyone else who knows me says, "I'm sure you will work things out". News flash, everyone: I am not working this out!'

'What about professional help?'

Ouch.

Maggie took a moment to compose herself.

'What, like a therapist or something?'

'Perhaps. A coach might be useful, depending on the help you are after.'

Excellent, she thinks I'm a failure too!

'Am I so terrible that I need coaching?'

'Engaging a coach doesn't make you terrible, and there is nothing wrong with asking for help. It's a sign of strength. You said you are out of your depth. So, how do you change the situation? If you were unwell, you would go to a doctor. Why not go to a professional for help in finding a new approach?'

'I guess that makes sense. I still feel useless, though.'

'Plenty of people seek help for stuff like this.'

'Sure, but I don't know any. Do you?'

'Yes, me.'

'You are the most competent, together person I know. What do you mean, you seek help?'

'I use a coach.'

'A coach?'

'Yes. Someone who listens to my concerns and asks questions to help me change how I am seeing things. Lots of people receive coaching. Even our Vice President has a coach.'

'Are you for real? He is confident and competent, and on top of his game. That's why he is Vice President! He doesn't need help.'

'He is a human, like the rest of us. He finds coaching valuable.'

I never realised people ask for professional help for different reasons.

'Would a coach help me?'

'Perhaps, if you want help and are prepared to learn. Coaching is a lot of hard work. You will need to put the effort in to get results, and that includes being willing to learn and change. Don't think, though, that a coach will "fix" you. Coaching is not about being "fixed". A coach won't see you as broken, so they won't be looking to "fix" you. You will learn to shift your perceptions of life and create new strategies for approaching challenges. If you are after a therapist, then coaching is not for you. Coaches aren't therapists. You need to choose what will work for you and your specific situation. If you think coaching is for you, then as long as you are prepared to do the work, it can be rewarding and very empowering.'

'Well, it sounds full on, but also better than sticking things out and not changing anything.'

'Oh good, you have moved to seeing new possibilities.'

Silence.

'Olivia, should I do this?'

'Your choice. My point is you are not alone. There are people who can help you.'

'Let's say I wanted a coach. Where would I find one?'

Olivia paused before saying, 'Don't get mad, but I have already found one who sounds like an excellent match for you.'

Trust Olivia to be prepared with an answer.

'What?'

'I did some research, just in case. I wasn't sure my coach would be a good fit for you, but I have found someone who sounds perfect. His name is Alex.'

So typical of Olivia. Although perhaps this is a positive thing. Olivia has taken the first step for me.

'And if I didn't want you to find me a coach?'

'I knew you would appreciate me making it easier for you.'

Maggie half chuckled and half sighed.

'You are unbelievable! Are you able to send me Alex's details?'

'I'll message them to you in a few minutes. Now, how are you?'

'I'm a mess. But I guess I am now a mess with some hope.'

'Ah, a step forward.'

'I hate being this way, Olivia.'

'I hate seeing you this way, Mags. Look, this job you've taken on is enormous, and I know it's not what you expected when you joined us. Don't be so hard on yourself. You just need some new strategies. That doesn't make you wrong; it just makes you human.'

'I guess I'll give coaching a go then.'

'Great! And remember, it's okay to ask for help.'

Until the coach sees how useless I am...

Through her tears, Maggie asked, 'Olivia, do you really think coaching will help me?'

'I am confident it will. In any case, anything has to be better than what's happening now.'

You've got me there.

'True. Well, thanks for the chat. I should pull myself together and get some work done.'

'Any time, Mags. I'll text you Alex's contact details.'

Less than five minutes after the call ended, Maggie's phone sounded.

Ah, Olivia's text with Alex's details.

Later, Maggie sat in silence. As she stared at Olivia's message, she considered her next steps.

Can a coach help me? What if I look silly? What if this is just who I am?

Enough! I will shift my mindset.

I will turn this around.

I am going to ask for help.

The Learning

The stories we tell ourselves

The words we say to ourselves become the stories from which we live. This can happen without us realising it. We attach emotions to our internal voices and accept those voices as 'the truth'. In doing so, we give power to our thoughts and emotions. What our mind creates, we become. Before we realise it, our chatter gains control over us, and we are travelling a road of suffering and self-judgement. This is happening to Maggie in her new job. She is having many conversations with herself, creating a cycle of being and doing that isn't helpful.

In *The Untethered Soul*, Michael A. Singer (2007) says our internal chatter is something we *hear* and not something we have to *be*. Our chatter helps us make meaning of our world, but only we can let it be our meaning of who we are. When we separate our chatter from who we are, we draw a boundary between what we say to ourselves and how we act in life. This allows us to choose how our thoughts influence our interactions with the world. We can listen to the voices while holding the power of choice.

Whether positive or negative, our thoughts and chatter can only influence us if we give them the authority to do so. This brings the management of our internal chatter down to two key steps:

1. Listen to what we are saying to ourselves.
2. Choose the level of authority we want to give these thoughts and words.

In the flow of life, we choose our actions without realising we are doing so. This is part of being human. Our prior learning about how to be in life sits in the background, informing us while we operate on autopilot. We make choices without realising, and we act from those choices. We listen to what our mind is saying and use those words to blindly create our life. Without noticing the chatter, we don't realise how much it informs our actions. Our human autopilot compares our experiences with our past learning to make choices with no deliberate input from us.

When we are oblivious to the choices behind our actions, we limit our influence over whether or not our actions will serve us. We operate on autopilot, unaware of what our actions are creating.

By paying attention to our internal thoughts and chatter, we notice how we are seeing the world and what we are doing with our interpretations. With awareness of what is happening, we can choose what we want to happen and whether we give our thoughts the authority to create for us.

Maggie's experience highlights how we can suffer when our actions don't serve us. Her silent, unknown choices were not useful, and her thoughts and actions appeared to be causing her pain and suffering. In *Unbinding: The Grace Beyond Self*, Kathleen Dowling Singh (2017) provides a link between suffering and ignorance, describing ignorance as 'the absence of paying attention' rather than a moral judgement. Singh claims that when we bring our self-view into our interactions, we become ignorant about what else exists, focusing on our personal perception of the world. We operate from habit, not noticing how we are seeing the world. Singh refers to this as 'ingraining the choice not to see'. We run on autopilot in our interactions, making blind choices from how we are, not from how the world exists. Instead of making deliberate choices for responding to the world, our ingrained 'choice not to see' leads to our responses choosing us, informed by our prior learning. This can cause pain and suffering that we mistake for reality.

We attach stories, moods and emotions to our experiences of life. Our body, home to everything that is us, is also the home of our stories (language), moods and emotions. When we choose not to see, we remove choice from the language, moods and emotions that we allow our body to absorb. Our suffering can affect our physical and mental wellbeing.

Time-out to practise

Identify a situation you are finding challenging.

1. What is your internal chatter telling you about yourself in the situation?

2. What is your internal chatter telling you about others in the situation?

3. How are you giving authority to your internal chatter?

4. What are you feeling in your body as you listen to this chatter?

5. What choices did you not realise you were making in the situation?

A new way forward

In our story, Maggie wants to change. Her thoughts and approach are not helping her, and she wants a different way forward. Maggie started by declaring the issue: *I can't keep going like this. I will break.*

But what is a declaration?

According to the *Cambridge Online Dictionary*, a declaration is:

- an announcement, often one that is written and official

- an official or public statement about something, or the act of making a statement.

A declaration is a statement of how things are or will be. Maggie's declaration was verbal, although also private. This declaration allowed her to see that something wasn't working for her and acknowledge that she wanted her path to change.

In *Language and the Pursuit of Happiness,* Chalmers Brothers (2005) claims declarations make new things possible, giving us the power to change our world by shifting our perspectives, rules and actions to bring forth new results. The question is, how can a simple statement in language produce new results? The answer lies in how humans use language.

Humans can use language to describe what already exists in the world. For example, the statement 'this is a table' describes an object that already exists in the world as a table. Brothers (2005) refers to this as the world existing first, with the words only existing because the world exists. Because an object exists as a table, the statement 'this is a table' also exists.

We also use language to describe how we interpret life or how we want life to be. When we do this, we are doing what Brothers (2005) suggests is speaking the words to create the world. For example, I might think a table is ugly. You might see it as a stunning table. The table doesn't exist in the world as either ugly or stunning. We spoke the table into existence in *our* world as ugly or stunning by declaring it as ugly or stunning. In the world, however, the table exists only as a table. This is how declarations create and make new things possible. Our words create something that didn't exist in the world previously.

Maggie demonstrated the creative aspect of declarations when she declared the changes she wanted to make in her life. Because she spoke these words, albeit privately, change became possible for her:

- *I will shift my mindset.*
- *I will turn this around.*
- *I am going to ask for help.*

When Maggie experienced the pain and suffering of her new job, the above actions did not exist in her world as actions she would take. It was only in declaring how life would be that she made these actions possible. Her declarations created a new path for Maggie, making new outcomes available to her.

We make declarations in our everyday life, often without awareness. This includes declarations such as what time we will get up for the day, what we will wear, and how we will treat the staff at the café. Each of our declarations creates our existence in the world. We say the words, privately or publicly, and the words create our world. None of us existed today as wearing what we are wearing until we declared it. Even if we wore our pyjamas for the day, that happened because we declared to ourselves that is what we would do. We weren't created as existing in our pyjamas for the day; we created that outcome by declaring that we would stay in our pyjamas. Likewise, none of us existed today as being kind or mean to the staff at the café. We created that reality when we, perhaps silently, declared to ourselves how we would treat the staff. We may not have even realised what we were saying to ourselves or what we were creating. With or without our awareness, our language creates our reality.

Figure 2: *Declarations make new things possible and change what will happen in our future*

Figure 2 provides an example of how we declare a meal into existence. Lasagne for dinner exists when we declare we will have lasagne for dinner. Until then, we could have anything for dinner, and lasagne for dinner doesn't exist.

A declaration must have authority if it is to be carried out. Those hearing the declaration will provide authority based on how they see the world. For example, if you declare that you will cook meat lasagne for a friend who doesn't eat meat, they may choose not to give authority to your declaration.

Maggie declared her new approach to herself, suggesting she needs her own authority if she wants a new way forward. While this may seem odd, it is significant. If we are not aware of the need to give ourselves permission to act on our personal declarations, we will prevent ourselves from taking action.

In *Human Design: discover the person you were born to be,* Chetan Parkyn (2009) suggests that authority is being able to take charge of our life, place trust in ourselves and act promptly and confidently. The *Cambridge Online Dictionary* links authority to permission. We can say that we give ourselves authority when we give ourselves permission to own our lives and place trust in our choices and actions. But how do we give ourselves authority?

Our ability to give ourselves authority comes from the way we use language, the moods and emotions we find ourselves in, and how we embody all of these. When we are not giving authority to ourselves, useful questions to ask are:

- What stories am I telling myself that prevent me from giving authority to myself?
- What stories (language) would help me give authority to myself?
- What moods and emotions are present that are preventing me from giving authority to myself?
- What moods and emotions would help me give authority to myself?
- Where are my stories, moods and emotions sitting in my body?
- How are my stories, moods and emotions sitting in my body?
- How could I shift my body to accommodate new stories, moods and emotions, and in so doing, help me give authority to myself?

A New Year's resolution is one example where we may not give ourselves authority and, therefore, not achieve. For example, we may declare we will change careers this year but not give ourselves the authority required to move forward and change careers. We said we would do it. We want to do it. Yet, without giving ourselves authority, we don't allow ourselves to do it.

Time-out to practise

Consider a time recently when things weren't going as expected, and you wanted to change the direction so you could achieve a different outcome:

1. What declarations did you make?
2. What authority did you give yourself to enact the declaration?
3. Where did you have difficulty in giving yourself authority?
4. What new way forward did your declarations create?
5. How did this new way forward align with your intentions?
6. How will you pay more attention to your declarations in future?

Declarations without awareness

We don't always realise when we are making declarations. This makes sense. No one teaches us about declarations, so how can we appreciate we are making them? The irony, however, is that declarations create a new future for us; they create our reality. If we are not aware that we are making a declaration, how do we choose the future we are creating? How do we create a reality that serves us?

Imagine you are in a cycle of declaring hatred. In that case, you may also be in a cycle of creating a future that doesn't meet your expectations. However, if you aren't aware of your declarations and their impact, how would you know what you are creating? And how would you know how to change what you are creating?

When we aren't aware of how we are using our declarations, we remove choice from what we are creating. Awareness enables choice. From a place of awareness, we can decide our reality.

Time-out to practise

Choose a recent conversation for your reflection.

1. What declarations did you make without awareness?
2. What did these declarations create?
3. How did the outcomes serve you?

Declarations change our future

Maggie declared that she was experiencing challenges in her work situation. In doing so, she acknowledged the misalignment between what she was creating and what she wanted to create. Next, Maggie declared the new actions she wanted to take. Together, these two steps form a key component of the six-step process described in this book.

At the beginning of each coaching conversation in this book, Maggie declares her challenge. Then, at the end of the conversation, she declares her new way forward. This enables her to acknowledge what is not serving her and find a new path that does.

For now, Maggie has given authority to her declaration and is ready to act. She is ready to change how she is seeing the world.

Time-out to practise

Choose a situation you assess as not working for you.

1. What declarations would help you move the situation in a different direction?

Declarations, stories, moods and emotions, and body

Each combination of our language, moods and emotions, and body will affect how we make and enact declarations. We have already talked about declarations and stories being elements of language. But what are moods and emotions, and how do each of our language, moods and emotions sit in our body?

In *The Happiness Trap: Stop Struggling, Start Living*, Dr Russ Harris (2007) likens emotions to a storm and moods to an overcast day. This paints a picture of emotions being an in-the-moment response to how we are seeing the world and moods being an overarching view of the world.

Moods are often long-lasting. They inform our interpretations and lead our actions. In *Learning to Learn and the Navigation of Moods: The Meta-Skill for the Acquisition of Skills*, Gloria P. Flores (2016) suggests that moods sit in the background, providing an often-unseen lens for how we see the world. When we are unaware that a mood is present, we can't know what lens it provides us for life. And when we don't know what lens we are looking through, we have no way of knowing how it drives our worldview and actions.

Sieler (2007) describes a model he calls 'Some Basic Moods of Life'. He notes these moods are only *some* and by no means the *only* moods for life, hence the model's title. Sieler's model adopts the interpretation that we all have three primary ways we feel about our experiences in life:

1. I feel like this situation definitely cannot be changed.
2. I feel like this situation could be changed (possibility).
3. I feel like there is uncertainty about what might happen.

Sieler suggests that we can respond to each of the ways we are feeling in one of two ways:

1. I am pushing away (opposing) how I am feeling about the situation.
2. I am accepting how I am feeling about the situation.

Each combination of feelings and responses creates a mood, such as resentment, resignation, anxiety, acceptance, ambition and wonder, as shown in Figure 3.

I am...	I feel like...		
	...this situation definitely cannot be changed	...it is possible this situation could be changed	...there is uncertainty about what might happen
...pushing away how I am feeling	The mood I am creating is RESENTMENT	The mood I am creating is RESIGNATION	The mood I am creating is ANXIETY
...accepting that I feel the way I feel	The mood I am creating is ACCEPTANCE	The mood I am creating is AMBITION	The mood I am creating is WONDER

Figure 3: *Some Basic Moods of Life Model (Sieler, 2007)*

We can create moods with or without awareness. When we don't notice how we are feeling about a situation or how we are responding to that feeling, we unwittingly create a mood to underpin our existence. When that happens, we view life through a specific mood lens without realising it. Yet if we can create one mood based on how we respond to what we are feeling, it must also be possible to create new moods. Once we become aware of where our moods are not serving us, we can ask ourselves:

- What am I seeing as unable to be changed? How is that helping me?
- What am I seeing as possible to change? How is that helping me?
- What am I seeing as uncertain? How is that helping me?
- What am I pushing away or accepting? How is that helping me?
- What would be useful to accept or push away that I am not accepting or pushing away?
- What new moods would I like to create?

Emotions are a response to a specific event. For example, winning an award may lead to joy or pride. Seeing a loved one treated unfairly may lead to anger. Emotions are short-lived and often more obvious than moods. In *The Unopened Gift: A primer in emotional literacy,* Newby and Núñez (2017) claim each emotion has:

- a story we tell ourselves while in the emotion
- an action the emotion inclines us to take
- a purpose.

When we experience emotions, we can understand them further by noticing what they are telling us, what action we feel inclined to take, and why the emotion might be present.

Our language, moods and emotions live in our body. This contributes to our Way of Being and the actions available for us to take. In *Suffering is Optional*, Gail Brenner (2018) claims that welcoming our feelings shows us how they are living in our body. Further, Brenner (2018) offers that our ability to welcome our physical sensations provides us with a gateway to presence, claiming we can become caught up in the story about our feelings, removing our attention from the present. Brenner (2018) also suggests we can find freedom when we allow feelings to be present by noticing the physical sensations they create.

In *Embodied Leadership*, Pete Hamill (2013) claims our culture has led us to believe that our mind, or who we are, is detached from our body. This suggests we have separated who we are from our felt experience of being alive and being who we are. We have a body, and we experience life, but our culture doesn't always enable us to feel the experience of life in our body. Hamill (2013) proposes the development of our understanding of an embodied mind or self requires us to see ourselves differently in the world. According to Hamill (2013), we can no longer see our body as a machine that carries the mind around. Instead, we must understand the body as an integrated part of who we are, our self.

When we see our body as part of our being, we can also see how our body helps to inform the actions we take from our moods and emotions. In particular, we want to understand how our language, moods and emotions, and body contribute to the outcomes we achieve from our declarations. Cues we may notice in our body include:

- The position of our legs and feet. Are our feet planted firmly on the ground, or are they elsewhere? Are our knees touching, or is there some distance between them?
- Our posture. How centred is our body? Is our spine elongated or compressed? Are we standing tall, or do we have a diminished posture?
- Our breathing. Is our breathing fast or slow? Are our breaths deep or shallow?
- Tension, rigidity or ease. Where might we be feeling tense, rigid or at ease? For example, is there tension and discomfort around the shoulders and neck or do those areas feel relaxed and comfortable?
- Torso. Is our torso open or concave?
- Sensations in our body. How does our body feel? What are we sensing throughout our body?

In Table 1, we explore how different combinations of language (stories), moods and emotions, and body contribute to different outcomes while making a declaration using the simple yet relatable example of washing the dishes. The table offers an example of possible outcomes and is not a definitive list. You may be able to think of other outcomes that are not listed.

Declaration: I will wash the dishes.

Mood or Emotion	Story you might be telling yourself	Body	Potential outcome
Resentment	• I do not believe I can change this situation and I reject that belief. • I hate washing the dishes. • It is unfair that no one else ever does the dishes. • I shouldn't have to do this.	• Reduced height. • Tense shoulders and jaw and tightness in stomach. • Concave chest.	• You enact the declaration from a place of wanting to get even, not considering how you are affecting others. • Storming around and making others suffer. • Making the declaration without considering its effect on those around you.
Resignation	• It is possible that I could get out of helping with the dishes, but I don't think that is really going to happen. • Why even bother? No one will appreciate it. • No one else is going to do it, so I might as well do it.	• Heavy, lethargic. • Reduced length. • Hunched shoulders. • Concave chest. • Shallow breathing. • Sighing.	• Resignation directs you towards giving up, so you may not enact the declaration. • Wondering why you are even bothering. • You are self-absorbed. • If you wash up, it's as though you are surrendering. But you feel you have no choice and are not committed to the outcome.

WHAT IF LIFE CAME WITH A USER GUIDE?

Declaration: I will wash the dishes.			
Mood or Emotion	**Story you might be telling yourself**	**Body**	**Potential outcome**
Anxiety	• Something may harm me, but I don't know what it is. • I will not cope if the worst happens. • I must protect myself from harm.	• Posture is diminished to reduce the possibility of being noticed. • Chest is tight and concave. • Shallow breathing. • Eyes looking down.	• You wash up but are withdrawn and focused on keeping yourself safe while you're doing it. • Your thoughts and words could be defensive and self-protecting.
Acceptance	• What has happened, has happened. I don't like it, but I know I can't change it. • It is what it is. • These are the boundaries I must work within.	• Sitting and moving with ease. • Relaxed muscles in face, neck, back, arms, shoulders and legs, yet also ready to act. • Relaxed attention. • Loose fingers. • Relaxed mouth and jaw • Nostril breathing, breath low in belly.	• You wash the dishes without complaint, understanding that it is what it is.
Ambition	• I can make a difference and I am going to do so. • Let's go! • Let's make this happen!	• Posture upright. • Expanded and open chest. • Eyes looking out to the world, looking for possibilities.	• You are keen to wash the dishes and achieve an outcome. • You are open to any possibilities that may appear.

Declaration: I will wash the dishes.			
Mood or Emotion	**Story you might be telling yourself**	**Body**	**Potential outcome**
Wonder	• The world is fascinating, and I want to find out all I can about it. • I want to explore. • I wonder what will happen?	• Open and relaxed body. • Wide-eyed. • Ease in posture. • Ready to engage.	• You will wash the dishes and be willing to explore while doing so. • You realise this could lead to lots of conversations. • You are willing to see what happens.
Gratitude	• I love helping because dinner was such a gift. • It is wonderful to be a part of this.	• Uplifted. • Open torso. • Full chest. • Deep, steady breathing.	• You enact the declaration without judgement. • You work from a place of gratitude for the gifts that led you to want to wash the dishes.
Joy	• Life is worth celebrating.	• Deep breathing. • Elongated spine. • Energy flowing through the body. • Head and chin held high, arms wide.	• If you wash the dishes, you will see it as an opportunity to celebrate while remaining open to those around you.
Pity	• This person needs my support.	• Very slow breathing in heart region. • Shoulders rounded. • Lethargic. • Head down.	• You wash the dishes because you see others as needing your help and support.

WHAT IF LIFE CAME WITH A USER GUIDE?

Declaration: I will wash the dishes.			
Mood or Emotion	Story you might be telling yourself	Body	Potential outcome
Obligation	• I have no choice. • I have to do it.	• Weighted. • Slumped shoulders. • Concave torso. • Shallow, slow breathing.	• You wash the dishes, but only out of a sense of obligation. • You may not engage, closing yourself to others.

Table 1: *Our language, moods and emotions, and body underpin our declarations*[1,2]

1 Moods in this table are sourced from Sieler (2007)

2 Emotions in this table are sourced from Newby and Núñez (2017) and Newby and Watkins (2019)

As you can see from Table 1, our language, moods and emotions, and body influence our declarations and how we enact them. A useful approach may be to explore how you would make a declaration from each of the different combinations of language, moods and emotions, and body listed in Table 1.

- What outcomes might you achieve?
- How are the outcomes you are imagining different to the potential outcomes listed in Table 1? Remember, we each see the world differently, so it is possible you will see different outcomes from those listed.

When we choose our declarations and the language, moods and emotions, and body accompanying them, we are choosing the future we want to create.

Time-out to practise

Consider a declaration that would move you in a different direction.

1. When you imagine making the declaration, what is going on in:
   a. your language?
   b. your moods and emotions?
   c. your body?

2. How is the combination of language, moods and emotions, and body helping you?

3. What combination of language, moods and emotions, and body would help you make this declaration?

A Deeper Reflection

Choose a situation in your life that you would like to change.

1. What stories are you telling yourself about the situation?
2. How are your stories helping you?
3. What actions did you take without choosing?
4. What have you declared?
5. How have the declarations helped you?
6. What declarations have not been helpful?
7. Why have the declarations not been helpful?
8. What declarations have you not made?
9. What declarations are you going to make to help change the situation?
10. What combination of language, moods and emotions, and body would help you make a declaration that serves you?
11. Consider practising the declaration in front of a mirror.

Key Points

- We do not have to be what our internal chatter says we are.
- Humans often run on autopilot, with our actions choosing us rather than us choosing our actions.
- When we pay attention to our language, moods and emotions, and body, we create choice in our actions.
- Declarations create our future for us, even if we don't realise it.
- When we declare our challenges, we are acknowledging the misalignment between what we are creating and what we want to create.
- Declarations can provide us with a new way forward and a new future.
- We must have authority to enact our declarations.

CHAPTER 2

How do I ask for help?

The Story

For years, Dolly's Café has been one of Maggie's favourites. She loves sitting outside, especially at this time of year, the tree-lined street an absolute delight in all its spring-time glory.

'So?' asked Olivia.

'So what?'

'Have you contacted Alex yet?'

'No.'

'Right.'

Maggie's gaze darted towards Olivia. 'What do you mean, "Right"?'

'I guess I just assumed you would want to get help.'

'But...'

'This is your choice, Mags. I won't force you. But if I were in your shoes, I would make the call.'

Oh, my goodness. This is hard for me, Olivia. Don't push me.

'I am not sure how to call a stranger and say, "Hi, I am Maggie. I am an emotional wreck with no self-confidence. I spend my days crying because I am incompetent at everything. Can you help me?"'

'Stop judging yourself; just dial the number.'

It's easy to judge myself when everything is going so wrong.

'I need to prepare for this. I hate talking to people on the phone. And what if Alex is busy?'

'When I am busy, I don't answer my phone. Maybe Alex will do the same.'

Olivia always has an answer.

Another long sigh. 'You will not let up, will you?'

'Maggie, I care. And I am worried about you.'

I understand, but there's no need to pressure me.

'And I am grateful for your concern. It's just hard.'

'I understand. Didn't I give you an email address for Alex? Why not email? That way, you can avoid the phone while also taking a step forward.'

Maggie's hands dropped to her lap.

'Okay.'

'You'll email Alex?'

Do I have a choice?

Maggie sighed and shook her head from side to side, mimicking Olivia as she spoke. 'Yes, I will email Alex.'

Later, at home, Maggie started typing.

Oh, my goodness. I feel ill. I want a solution, but I am ashamed to admit my challenges to a stranger.

Maggie kept changing her email, searching for the right words. In the end, she went for honesty.

Hi Alex,

My name is Maggie. I am struggling at work and my friend Olivia recommended you as someone who may be able to help me. I lack confidence and doubt myself most of the time. I am stuck. I can't break the cycle and I don't know what to do.

My old ways of coping are no longer working. Do you offer coaching that would help?

Thank you.

Regards,

Maggie.

Maggie squeezed her eyes shut as she hit send on the email.

> *If I can't see myself hitting send, I can't stop myself from emailing. I must take this step. I need help.*

The Learning

Making a request

Maggie could not find a way out of her challenging work situation without asking for help. This is neither bad nor wrong. Asking for help can be useful; it removes barriers and helps to reduce our personal suffering.

Brothers (2005) refers to asking for help as 'making a request'. He suggests we make requests when we identify that the future will unfold in an undesirable way. When we don't want the future that we are heading towards and determine that we require help if we are to achieve our preferred future, making a request is the logical next step.

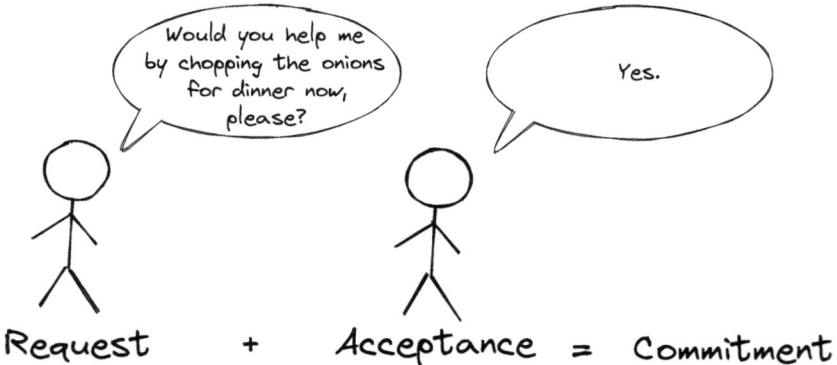

Figure 4: *When someone accepts a request, a commitment exists*

When we make a request of someone, we can expect the person to either accept or decline the request. As shown in Figure 4, acceptance of a request creates a commitment. If Alex accepts Maggie's request for help, a commitment will exist. We expect action when a commitment exists. It is the responsibility of the person who accepted the request to fulfil it.

Time-out to practise

Choose a situation where you are stuck.

1. What requests would help you move forward?
2. To whom will you make these requests?

Asking for help isn't always easy

At first, Maggie hesitated to contact Alex. She made excuses, including worrying about how Alex might judge her and whether he might be too busy. In *All you have to do is ask*, Wayne Baker (2020) claims many of us find it terrifying to ask for help, although doing so is often the action most likely to lead us towards success.

The likelihood of receiving help without making a request is slim. After all, how can others know what we need unless we explicitly tell them? Baker cites studies showing up to 90% of help provided in the workplace only occurs after a request is made, suggesting that not asking for help can be self-limiting and even self-destructive.

We each hold stories about what making a request means for us in any given situation. Sometimes, these stories prevent us from asking for help. This leads to unwanted outcomes as we hold ourselves back from taking a step in our preferred direction. When we hold ourselves back by not making requests, we impose constraints or limitations, restricting what is possible. Sometimes, we can lead ourselves toward an unwanted future by not declaring that we will ask for help.

Why does asking for help pose such a challenge? Let me explain. We create meaning from our experiences in life. This includes creating meaning about asking for help. For example, while growing up in my family, we were expected to help others. Yet, we would never ask for help ourselves. For a long time, I would offer to help others but would never request help for myself. Based on my earlier life experiences, my standard made me think asking for help was wrong. It took me years to achieve a change in this standard. Once the standard changed, the story I associated with asking for help also changed. Now, I can ask for help without guilt.

Time-out to practise

Let's explore what asking for help means to you.

1. What stories do you hold about asking for help?
2. How do these stories support you in asking for help?
3. How do these stories limit your ability to ask for help?
4. What would it take to shift your limiting stories about asking for help?

Requests, language, moods and emotions, and body

Our language, moods and emotions, and body play a role in the effectiveness of our requests. Table 2 shows a request of 'May I borrow your car on Thursday?' made from different combinations of language (specifically stories), moods and emotions, and body. Each will produce different outcomes, and not all outcomes will be useful. The outcomes listed in Table 2 are only some outcomes, not the only outcomes. The table is an example and not a definitive list.

Request: May I borrow your car on Thursday?			
What mood or emotion underpins this request?	**What stories do you associate with this request?**	**What body do you associate with this request?**	**What is the likely outcome?**
Shame	• It is wrong to ask for help. • I should not be troubling others.	• Head hanging down. • Shoulders slumped. • Concave torso. • Shallow breathing.	• You don't make the request. • You don't hold yourself as legitimate when making the request.

Acceptance	• I cannot do this alone and need help to move forward.	• Relaxed. • Open torso. • Elongated spine. • Slow breathing.	• You make the request, accepting you are legitimate in doing so.
Anxiety	• What if they are too busy? • What if they don't want to help me? • What if they don't want to say yes but feel obliged?	• Tightening through the body and neck. • Uncomfortable sensations in the stomach. • Withdrawn. • Fast, shallow, upper diaphragmatic breathing.	• You worry about what might happen, and this prevents you from making the request.
Curiosity	• I wonder what we can create if I ask for help? • I wonder whether I can help them on another occasion?	• Open torso. • Full chest. • Energised: the energy in your body is moving you forward. • Alert. • Regular, relaxed breathing, albeit slightly faster than normal.	• You make the request, searching for what is possible as you do so.

Table 2: *How our language, moods and emotions, and body affect us asking for help*

As Table 2 shows, the combination of our language, moods and emotions, and body either helps or limits us in making requests. We can explore what is happening by asking ourselves:

- What stories am I telling myself about making this request?
- What emotions have I attached to my stories?
- How is my body preventing me from making requests?
- What would help me make this request?

Time-out to practise

Consider a request you want to make but can't.

1. What stories, moods and emotions, and body are preventing you from making the request?
2. What stories, moods and emotions, and body would support you in making the request?

What happens when a request is missing or not fulfilled?

In *How the Way We Talk Can Change the Way We Work: Seven Languages for Transformation,* Robert Kegan and Lisa Laskow Lahey (2001) claim we complain about what we care about. They propose a 'river of our caring' underpins our complaints, drawing the connection that what we care about equates to what we commit ourselves to. They suggest we can reduce complaining by speaking from a place of commitment.

One way we can create a commitment is for a listener to accept a request. Since speaking from a place of commitment reduces our complaints, we can conclude that making requests helps reduce complaints. This implies that complaints will increase when we have missing requests.

Brothers (2005) proposes that requests help us shift to a preferred future. If we don't make a request, we may not see a shift to our preferred future. If we care about this future, chances are we will complain when those outcomes don't eventuate.

One example of a complaint is: 'My family never helps with the dishes.' To remove the complaint, the secret is to find the missing commitment. Why? Because if we can understand what commitment is missing, we can establish what request is missing. In this example, the missing commitment might be to help with the dishes. What request would create this commitment? Perhaps a request for ongoing help with the dishes would support you in turning the situation around.

When we develop an awareness of our missing requests, we position ourselves to make those requests. When we make requests and a commitment exists, we can continue in our chosen direction, holding others to account for fulfilling their commitments. If a request is not fulfilled, it is helpful to have a conversation to address the complaint and reach a useful outcome.

Time-out to practise

Consider a situation that is causing you to complain.

1. What do you care most about in this situation?
2. What commitments are missing?
3. What requests would help to create these commitments?
4. What stories, moods and emotions, and body would support you in making these requests?
5. What requests have you made that are yet to be fulfilled?
6. What language, moods and emotions, and body would support you in holding others to account for completing the request?

A Deeper Reflection

Reflect on a single goal you want to achieve this year.

1. What requests would help you achieve this goal?
2. To whom will you make these requests?
3. How will you use your language, moods and emotions, and body to support you in making the requests?
4. What requests have you not considered that might be useful?
5. What would help you make any missing requests?

Key Points

- Requests help move things forward when we need the help of others.
- When a request is accepted, a commitment exists.
- The person who accepted the request is responsible for honouring the commitment.
- Complaints arise when a request is missing or not fulfilled.
- Paying attention to our language, moods and emotions, and body helps us make effective requests.

WHAT IF LIFE CAME WITH A USER GUIDE?

CHAPTER 3

How can I learn to navigate the challenges of everyday life?

The Story

Maggie sat at her desk, looking at her task list. She felt better today. So far, things had gone according to plan, and her efforts seemed to be more effective.

I've made it to midday without crying, and I have ticked off several tasks – a better morning than most.

The phone paused Maggie's thoughts.

'Hello, Maggie speaking.'

'Oh, hello, Maggie. My name is Alex. You emailed me regarding coaching?'

Oh, gosh. I didn't expect the call so soon. I'm not prepared. What will I say?

'Hi Alex, how are you?'

'Well, thank you. And you?'

'I'm well, thanks.'

'Fantastic. So... how can I help?'

'I want to improve my confidence.'

Because I doubt myself so much and am incapable of doing anything.

'I can coach you on confidence and the other items in your email.

My approach differs from the more traditional coaching methods. Do you want to hear more before you decide whether we will work together?'

I should just book a session in before my nerves get the better of me and cause me to change my mind.

'Yes, I would like to hear more detail about your approach.'

Here I go, procrastinating again! But then again, it can't hurt to ask so I know what I'm up for.

'Okay, so my approach assumes everything we do results from how we use our language, and our moods and emotions, combined with how we embody those factors. The combination of these factors is called our Way of Being. I will help you understand how the way you are *being* influences your behaviour and actions. For example, if you have an issue with speaking up in meetings, we will seek to understand how you are using language, what moods and emotions you are working from, and how your body is storing your language, moods and emotions. We can seek new results by shifting the less useful elements of your language, moods and emotions, and body. Does this sound useful?'

It sounds different. But, hey, if I get results, who cares! I can't tell Olivia I didn't do it.

'Sounds… interesting.'

'This approach is powerful but can also be challenging, as it requires you to explore who you are being and becoming. You can only achieve this if you are open to learning. I will help you understand your contribution to your interactions and how you can create different results. I realise this might be unfamiliar and seem strange to you, but rest assured, we will work together. You are not alone.'

'Okay… I am sure there is plenty I am doing wrong. I'm happy to understand where I am going wrong and change those things.'

'It's not my job to judge you as right or wrong. You may notice judgements popping up for you throughout our conversations. We will explore them in a judgement-free way to help you understand how they may be helping or limiting you.'

At least Alex isn't assuming I am wrong. This 'being' stuff sounds weird, but I want things to change. I want to give it a go.

'I am open to learning and changing. I want to turn my current situation around and I will do whatever it takes.'

'What a great start! Would you like to book our first conversation?'

What Alex has told me so far has given me confidence that he knows what he is talking about. I really want to give this a shot.

'Yes, I would like to go ahead. Is there any chance of a late afternoon appointment sometime soon? I am free any afternoon.'

'Would 4:30pm Thursday work for you?'

'Perfect.'

Alex gave Maggie the address before ending the call.

Am I excited about a way forward or terrified of failure? I am unsure.

The Learning

Way of Being

You might recall from the Introduction that our language, moods and emotions, and body combine to form our Way of Being. We interpret the world and take action from our Way of Being. Our Way of Being makes some actions possible while making other actions less available. What does this mean?

As I write this, I am frustrated by an email I just received. Like many people, I am tempted to blame the email for my frustration. But the frustration is not coming from the email itself. The email is just a thing that has appeared in my life. My frustration is coming from how I am *interpreting* the email, and I am interpreting the email from my Way of Being. Different ways of being will create different interpretations of the same email. My Way of Being has led me to interpret the email as frustrating. The email itself is not frustrating. It's just an email. The frustration exists within me and my interpretations.

While reading the email, I tell myself stories about the email, the sender and myself. I tell myself the sender has created additional work for me. I attach the emotions of frustration and disappointment to my stories of the email. My shoulders are tense, and my posture is slumped, a sign of how my stories and emotions are being housed in my body.

I can learn from my Way of Being to understand my frustration and whether shifting it would be useful. This will help me understand why I am forming my interpretations of the email and whether changing those interpretations might be beneficial.

In previous chapters, we developed an awareness of how our language, moods and emotions, and body affect our declarations and requests. Together, these three areas form our Way of Being. We observe ourselves and the world from our Way of Being. Our Way of Being also informs our actions and behaviours. We will discuss our Way of Being in more detail in the next chapter. For now, it is important to understand that our Way of Being underpins how we interpret the world and guides what we do.

If we can see our Way of Being as a source of learning and become learners of our language, moods and emotions, and body, we can shift our actions and transform our interactions in life.

Time-out to practise

Pause what you are doing now and pay attention to your Way of Being.

1. What are you saying and thinking to yourself?
2. What moods and emotions are present?
3. What is happening within your body?

The importance of being a learner

Alex suggested Maggie approach their conversations as a learner, focusing on how she is being in her language, moods and emotions, and body.

In our current society, we link learning to books, education, information and resources to help us with 'knowing'. We treat knowledge as an object, making learning a process of 'acquiring knowledge'. This approach leads us to see 'being a learner' as a judgement because we assume learning is only required when we don't hold knowledge. In a society where knowledge is everything, 'not knowing' can bring fear, anxiety and shame. While declaring ourselves as learners may be useful, doing so is not always easy. Reviewing and rewriting our stories for what it means to be a learner helps counter any self-judgement.

In *From Knowledge to Wisdom: Essays on the Crisis in Contemporary Learning*, Julio Olalla (2004) claims that while our learning practices focus on gaining knowledge, we must go further and improve our ability to take action. This creates two new possibilities for our learning:

1. Knowledge becomes a measure of our ability to take action in the world rather than a measure of our knowing.
2. Since our actions are generated by our Way of Being, our Way of Being becomes a valuable area of learning.

When we focus our learning on our Way of Being, we can understand how we relate to the world and improve our ability to take action.

Time-out to practise

Consider something new you would like to learn.

1. What are you telling yourself about being a learner?
2. What is present in your language, moods and emotions, and body when you imagine being a learner in this activity?
3. How are your language, moods and emotions, and body helping you in being a learner?

Be-Do-Learn

In life, if we don't like the results we are achieving, we often change our actions. For example, a tennis player who loses a game may improve their serve. This shifts the tennis player's actions, not the Way of Being informing their actions. An improved serve is of limited help if the tennis player believes they are not good at tennis, for example. When we want to transform our behaviours, exploring and shifting our Way of Being is often more useful than changing our actions.

Figure 5 shows the Be-Do-Learn approach, which focuses is on how our Way of Being is enabling our actions. We explore how we are being to bring about what we are doing. This new information helps us learn what is or is not serving us and what would help generate our preferred outcomes. When we apply our learning to how we are being, we can shift our doing.

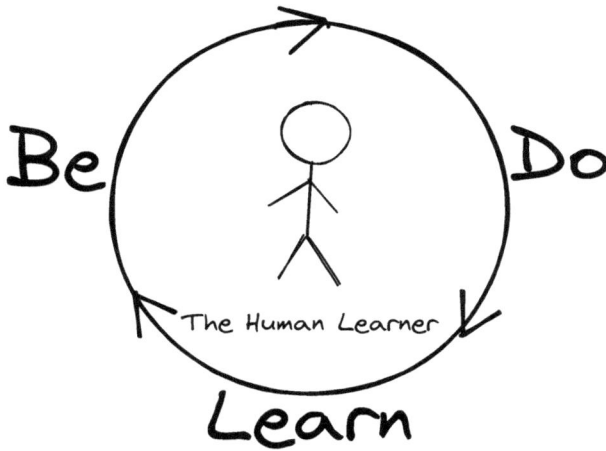

Figure 5: *The Be-Do-Learn approach*

To understand the Be-Do-Learn approach, let's consider an example, such as speaking in public. Many people have a fear of public speaking. Some ways to get around this fear might include rehearsing the speech repeatedly, avoiding public speaking, having slides with copious notes to ensure we don't forget anything or using cue cards. While each approach supports us in some way, they are all focused on the *doing* of public speaking. Yet we started from a place of *fearing* public speaking. As an emotion, fear is part of our Way of Being. If we haven't addressed the fear, the stories we are telling ourselves, or how both occur in our body, we haven't addressed our Way of Being around public speaking. So, what happens when the slideshow doesn't work or the cue cards are out of order? Our fearful Way of Being will most likely inform how we respond to the situation.

When we apply the Be-Do-Learn approach to the public speaking example, the first step will be to observe ourselves delivering the speech. We will *be* a certain way, in this case fearful, and *do* certain things, such as talking quickly, shaking or forgetting what the audience might want from us. This may or may not produce outcomes that serve us and our audience. But then we can *learn*. We can seek to understand what is going on in our Way of Being that is limiting or helping our doing. We can then apply our new learning to shift our Way of Being and generate new behaviours and actions.

When we only shift our doing, old ways of being still underpin our actions. This can create a struggle since our Way of Being influences our doing. However, when we shift our Way of Being, our actions and our Way of Being align, leading to more deliberate and lasting outcomes.

When we search within ourselves to understand how we are being in our interactions, we shift our focus from knowledge to taking effective action. Our Way of Being affects our doing, which also includes how we are as learners. This can happen without realisation.

Time-out to practise

Consider a situation that is not working well for you.

1. What is present in your language, moods and emotions, and body when you experience this situation?

   - What are you telling yourself about the situation?
   - What moods and emotions are present?
   - What sensations are present in your body?

2. What actions are you taking that are not helping?

3. What actions would you like to be taking?

4. What shifts in your language, moods and emotions, and body would help you take your preferred actions?

   - What would be helpful to tell yourself about the situation?
   - What moods and emotions would help you?
   - What sensations, posture and breathing would help you?

5. What would help or support you to make these shifts?

Our learning foes

In *Learning to Learn and the Navigation of Moods: The Meta-Skill for the Acquisition of Skills*, Gloria P. Flores (2016) suggests the assessments and standards we live by can unintentionally impede our ability to learn. This leads to what I call 'learning foes'.

Our learning foes are the elements of language, moods and emotions, and body that prevent us from learning. Authors such as Alan Sieler (2007) and author of *Connect: Affective leadership for effective results*, Lyn Boyer (2011), refer to these as 'enemies of learning'.

Our learning foes (or enemies of learning) include:

- acting as though we are already knowledgeable
- a view of 'I am in the right' or 'I know it all'
- anxiety about how others may judge us
- declarations that we are not capable enough to learn or can't do it
- not giving ourselves permission to learn
- emotions such as fear, doubt and arrogance
- impatience
- not being at peace with uncertainty
- not accepting new learning or holding on to old learning.

When present, our learning foes affect our ability to learn. We may want to learn how to interact with someone more resourcefully, but if we hold a view such as 'I am right' or 'I know it all', we limit what we view as possible. We can't change what we don't see as worthy of change.

Time-out to practise

Consider a skill you would like to improve.

1. What learning foes are present for you?
2. How do you think your learning foes are helping you? What stories are you telling yourself about them?
3. How are your learning foes limiting you?
4. What might help you shift your learning foes?

Our learning friends

In contrast to our learning foes, our learning friends help to bring forward new possibilities for learning. Our learning friends are the elements of language, moods and emotions, and body that support us in our learning. Sieler refers to our learning friends as 'allies of learning'. Some examples include:

- willingness and permission to say, 'i don't know'
- curiosity
- comfort and safety in declaring ourselves a learner
- being comfortable with not knowing
- willingness to seek new ways of taking action
- willingness to experience and understand uncomfortable thoughts, emotions and feelings
- persistence, humility, acceptance or patience.

Our learning friends help our view of the world to be less fixed. When we see our interactions with flexibility, we create choice.

Time-out to practise

Consider a situation where you are committed to being a learner.

1. What learning friends are present for you?
2. How are your learning friends helping you?
3. What other learning friends might be helpful for you?

A Deeper Reflection

Consider a situation that has not been going well for you:

1. What would it take to declare yourself a learner in this situation?
2. What elements of language, moods and emotions, and body are generating your current actions?
3. What learning friends and foes are present?
4. What elements of language, moods and emotions, and body would help you shift the situation?
5. What would help you shift your language, moods and emotions, and body?
6. How would you apply this new learning to shift your Way of Being and, therefore, the actions you are taking?

Key Points

- Our Way of Being is the combination of our language, moods and emotions, and body.
- Our Way of Being underpins all actions and behaviours.
- Exploring our Way of Being provides a valuable source of learning.
- We can be learners about our ability to take action; learning is not only about gaining knowledge.
- The Be-Do-Learn approach enables us to learn about our Way of Being so we can produce new actions (doing).
- Our learning foes prevent us from taking on new learning.
- Our learning friends help us take on new learning.
- Our Way of Being can affect our learning friends and foes.

CHAPTER 4

What is a Way of Being and why would I want to shift it?

The Story

Alex and Maggie were meeting for the first time in Alex's home office, which overlooked a lovely garden. Alex sat straight, shoulders back, palms in his lap, confident yet relaxed. Maggie fidgeted.

What if I am incompetent and unfixable?

Alex's words cut Maggie's internal chatter short.

'It's warm today, isn't it.'

Well, at least we are starting with small talk. I hope the session goes well. Oh, my goodness, what if I mess things up? What if we can't work together?

Returning her attention to Alex, Maggie responded, 'Yes, indeed. The weather forecast is for high temperatures until the weekend. It's going to be scorching!'

'There's my excuse for not gardening this week, then!' said Alex.

Maggie and Alex both gave a chuckle. There was a slight awkwardness when the chuckling stopped.

Alex spoke first, 'In your email, you said you are struggling with doubt and low self-esteem?'

Well, here goes...

'Yes, I always doubt myself. Doubt stops me from doing my job. I am stuck.'

Alex nodded before replying. 'Well, it's great you are acknowledging your challenges and seeking help. I am sure we can work through this together.'

'I hope so.'

'I gave you an overview on the phone, but would you like me to explain my approach in more detail?'

'Yes, please.'

I hope this works.

'Coaching helps people to shift their perspective and change what is possible. We each hold the ability to handle life's challenges within us. Sometimes, we just need help to access it. That's where I come in. I will ask questions to help you explore what is happening within you. We will work together to help you develop your own way forward, making it meaningful for you.'

'Sounds useful.'

What if I can't find a way forward?

Alex continued, 'At the beginning of each conversation, I will ask you to state your topic for the conversation. I won't give you answers. However, I will ask questions to help you clarify your experience. This will allow you to explore shifting your situation to something different. When you identify possibilities, choosing your actions becomes easier. We will end each conversation with a declaration of your chosen way forward. The intention is for you to find a path that makes sense to you. We can reflect on what happened when we meet for our next session. This is the process we will follow.'

I expected we would just talk. I didn't realise we would follow a process.

'So, our conversations will be about understanding what isn't working for me and finding new ways forward?' asked Maggie.

'Yes. As I said on the phone, my approach differs from traditional coaching methods because I don't focus so much on actions and goals. I focus on your Way of Being. I will help you discover what is happening in your Way of Being in the situations you describe. Each Way of Being allows different actions. Creating new actions will require you to understand and shift your Way of Being. Questions so far?'

I don't understand 'Way of Being'.

'Your approach sounds interesting. Can you give me more information about our Way of Being?'

'Of course. Our Way of Being is the interrelationship between our language, moods and emotions, and body. How we act comes from our Way of Being. New ways of being generate fresh actions.'

'Ah, yes, you mentioned some of that on the phone. I didn't connect with "Way of Being", though.'

'That's fine. You are always welcome to ask if you are unsure.'

'Thanks.'

Wow, Alex seems nice.

Alex continued. 'So, our language comprises our opinions, the stories we tell ourselves, and how we speak and listen to others and ourselves. Our moods and emotions tell us how we are interpreting the world. We don't realise it, but we are operating from moods and emotions in every given moment. Those moods and emotions help to inform the actions we take.'

That kind of makes sense. If I am angry, my behaviour differs from when I am happy.

'The last piece of the puzzle is our body. Our body is home to us: our thoughts, feelings, moods, emotions and everything happening within us. Whatever is within us will affect how we are using our body. This includes posture, breathing, body sensations and so forth.'

'Wow! Interesting!' Maggie said, wide-eyed.

Alex's approach sounds useful. Weird, but useful. Still, I will try anything. I just hope the process isn't too weird and gets results.

Alex smiled. 'Way of Being can be fascinating. We will explore shifting your language, moods and emotions, and body to help you achieve more useful outcomes.'

'Do we each have one Way of Being?'

'That's a good question. Overall, there may be a default Way of Being to guide our actions. We use different ways of being in interactions based on our perceptions. Things happen in our interactions that shift our being. For instance, if my phone rang now, my Way of Being might shift. When our interactions aren't working, we can choose to shift to more useful ways of being.'

I don't understand my Way of Being. And why must I? Why can't I just change my actions? Maybe I will ask…

'Why can't we just change the actions? It sounds easier.'

Maggie relaxed into the chair, tilting her head toward Alex with curiosity.

I hope that wasn't a silly question.

Alex smiled. 'Another good question! Our Way of Being specifies the actions available or not available to us. If we only change our actions, we could fall back on those less useful actions because our Way of Being hasn't changed. Also, our Way of Being generates our actions. Without changing our Way of Being, our actions may not change. Our preferred action may not be available from our current Way of Being.'

So, my Way of Being influences the actions I take? This is not quite what I expected from coaching.

Alex continued. 'Imagine setting the oven to 250 degrees Celsius to bake a cake from a recipe advising the oven to be at 180 degrees. If we maintain the oven at 250 degrees and adjust the time, we may produce an edible cake. We also may not. The most consistent results require us to understand oven temperature.'

Ah, I think I am starting to understand!

'Your analogy makes sense.'

'Fantastic! So, when we understand oven temperature, we can change the temperature to one that will produce an edible cake. Our Way of Being is the same. Our actions come from our Way of Being. We can try changing only our actions; however, the most consistent results will come from adjusting our Way of Being.'

I still don't understand where our Way of Being comes from.

'What creates our Way of Being?'

Look at me, asking questions!

'When we interact with the world, we learn rules for living. These rules may be subtle, or they might be more obvious. The rules come from our past: our culture, upbringing, society and life experience. We use this past learning in the present to create who we are being and becoming.'

So many new phrases for me to understand! How am I going to manage this?

'What do you mean by past learning?'

'Let me use an example. As a child, what is something that your parents taught you?'

Maggie pondered the question.

'To always use my manners.'

'Good one. And how does this inform your behaviour as an adult?'

Oh, my goodness, I am the person who says please and thank you all the time. Better to ask how manners don't inform my behaviour.

'I say please and thank you, even when doing so doesn't matter. I worry if I forget to say them, and I get frustrated when others don't use their manners.'

'Excellent. Manners are a good example of prior learning. Your behaviours as an adult are perhaps being informed by your learning of manners as a child. You still use the rules for manners society taught you, and you may also use this learning as a standard for judging others.'

Wait, aren't manners a good thing? Sounds like Alex is saying manners are bad.

Alex explained further. 'We use our prior learning, like your example of manners, in the present to create our future. This isn't wrong. Often, our learning has helped us for years. Lifetimes, even. We may arrive at a point where our learning isn't so useful. We may be unaware of how it informs us or even that our learning exists. We won't always be aware of what is behind our actions. Shifting our Way of Being means exploring our past learning and creating new learning to apply to our Way of Being.'

This keeps getting deeper. I'm intrigued yet nervous.

'I understand what you are saying, Alex, but there is so much information. How will I remember everything, and what if I can't use the ideas?'

'I understand this is new. You don't need to remember and use everything at once. We will work together. I'll help you discover new ways of interpreting and being, and you won't be alone. I'm sure you can do this. Shall we start?'

At least one of us has faith in me...

'Yeah, I guess so.'

Maggie's smile displayed a mix of curiosity, hope and resignation.

I am here now, so I guess I'd better seize the opportunity. I just hope this works.

The Learning

Our history is our foundation

In *Conversations for Action and Collected Essays: Instilling a Culture of Commitment in Working*, Fernando Flores (2012) calls humans 'historical beings', suggesting we embody the learning we take from life. This means the rules we learn for living life become a part of us, informing our choices at each moment and creating who we are in the future. Often, we may not be aware our rules exist. They sit in the background, informing our being and our doing. Our rules are our past, and our past is the foundation on which we build who we are being in life.

If life has taught us that pushing in front of someone in the supermarket queue is wrong, this learning can inform our actions when someone jumps the queue at the supermarket or even when we join a queue at the supermarket. Our thoughts, words, judgements and what we are feeling will all be influenced by this learning. We take action, perhaps unaware of how or why we are doing so. Our prior learning informs our judgements of ourselves and others based on our learning about queue jumping. We attach moods and emotions to our queue-jumping experience and house those in our body. When we respond, we do so in whatever way the combination of these areas allows.

Alex and Maggie discussed manners as an example of how our past learning is used to inform who we are being throughout our life. Teaching manners to children helps to achieve order by setting boundaries for behaviours. Beyond childhood, we never review this early learning. No one comes along later in life and says, 'Manners were a guide during your childhood. Now that you are an adult, you can use your learning about manners in whatever way works for you.' As a result, our past learning of manners remains, becoming an integral part of who we are. This early learning can then underpin everything we do. Our autopilot-based responses to people will include judgements informed by the learning of manners we have embodied in our past.

During the conversation, Maggie said she had learnt to see using manners as good or the right thing to do. Society has taught us that our manners show the standards by which we live. If we use our manners, then we must be good. How we use our manners underpins how we see ourselves and others. Have you ever caught yourself saying, 'They didn't even say thank you!' in disgust when someone hasn't thanked you for something? This is coming from your prior learning of manners. As another example, if you have ever said sorry for no reason, perhaps your early learning of manners contributed to this behaviour.

The rules set by our prior learning are not wrong. Most times, our learning has served us throughout the bulk of our life. However, our learning can limit us by informing our behaviours in unhelpful ways. For example, if we label everyone who never says please as a bad person, how will this affect our interactions with others?

We become ambassadors for ourselves when we are aware of how our history informs and influences us. Further, when we understand our rules and standards for living, we gain insight into how we measure ourselves and others. We empower ourselves by creating choices in how we interact.

Time-out to practise

Reflect on a recent time when you were annoyed about something.

1. What personal rules were you applying to this situation that led to you being annoyed?
2. How did the rules help?
3. How might it be useful to change your rules?

Way of Being

As Alex explained to Maggie, our history informs our Way of Being in the present, enabling us to take action to create our future. We aren't born with an awareness of our Way of Being or the actions our Way of Being allows. This suggests we can act without being aware of what we are doing and why. But what is our Way of Being?

In *Coaching to the Human Soul: Ontological Coaching and Deep Change: Vol. I* Sieler (2003) provides his interpretation of our Way of Being:

> '[…] Way of Being is an interrelationship between language, emotion and physiology […] In this interpretation, how we are at any point in time is a dynamic interplay between the three domains of human existence. How the world is for us will be shaped by our Way of Being; the world 'shows up' for us according to our Way of Being. In short, the results each of us obtains in life are greatly influenced by how we speak and listen, by our moods and emotions and by our body.'

Our Way of Being is the lens through which we observe and interact with the world. We perceive the world as our Way of Being allows. This includes how we perceive and interact with ourselves and with others. From our Way of Being, some actions and behaviours are available to us, while others are not.

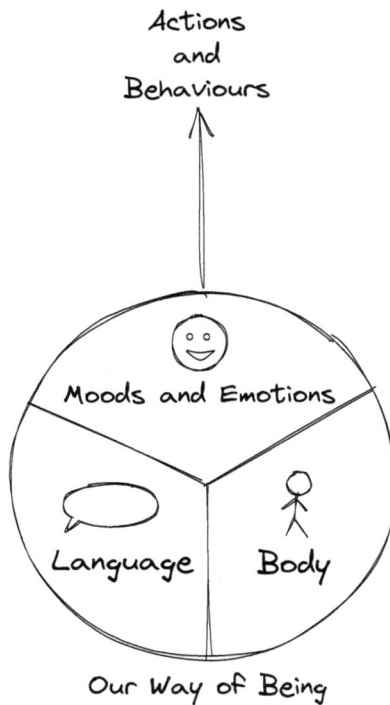

Figure 6: *Way of Being as a generator of actions and behaviours*

Figure 6 shows our Way of Being as a generator of our actions and behaviours. Our language, moods and emotions, and body define what we can and cannot do. This includes how we think, interpret, use our emotions, speak and listen.

Alex suggested to Maggie that understanding her Way of Being would be a key part of the coaching process. To understand our Way of Being, we need awareness of our language, moods and emotions, and body. But what does this mean? Let's break it down by examining the three parts that make up our Way of Being.

Language

How we speak, think, listen and interpret helps us make sense of the world. How we do each of these things, why we do them, and how they affect our view of the world are all a part of our language.

Imagine you are taking a friend to a medical appointment. You walk out to the car only to find the front driver's side tyre is flat. As you will need to replace the tyre, you know you will be late to collect your friend. Below are some examples of what you might say to yourself in this situation. Each will affect your Way of Being differently, which in turn will impact your experience of the flat tyre:

- Oh, the tyre is flat!
- I am so pleased I have a spare tyre.
- At least I can change a tyre. The tyre will be replaced in plenty of time.
- I wonder if I could catch a cab to my friend's place and drive to her appointment in her car?
- Now I am running late and am letting my friend down. I hate today!
- Why do these things always happen to me? Nothing I do ever works out how I want it to.
- My life is so unfair.
- Well, this has added fun and excitement to my morning!

Although we can choose what we say to ourselves in specific situations, our choices are often transparent to us, so we respond however our Way of Being allows. When we notice the stories we are telling ourselves, we can choose how to use those stories. For example, if a story of 'I can't do this' is not serving us, we can seek another more helpful story, such as 'I wonder what I can achieve?'

Time-out to practise

Consider a time when something didn't go according to plan.

1. What did you say to yourself?
2. How did your thoughts and words influence the actions you took?
3. If what you were saying wasn't helpful, how could you have shifted your language to something more helpful?

Moods and emotions

Moods and emotions are always present in us, even if we aren't aware of their presence. Our moods and emotions influence our perception of the world at each moment.

From our earlier example, some emotions accompanying the discovery of a flat tyre might include acceptance, anger, hilarity and self-pity. Each emotion will both influence and be influenced by our perceptions.

In our earlier example for language, we considered what we might say upon discovering a flat tyre. In Table 3, we choose one of those statements and explore how different emotions might influence how we respond.

What we are saying to ourselves: 'Oh no, the tyre is flat!'	
What mood or emotion is present?	**What actions are most likely?**
• Acceptance	• Stop worrying and find a solution.
• Anger	• Tell ourselves stories about how unfair the situation is, maybe lay blame or rant. The solution may come from a place of wanting to right a wrong.
• Hilarity	• Laugh, take joy from the situation, and find a solution.
• Self-pity	• Perhaps rely on someone else to help fix the situation.

Table 3: *Different emotions generate different ways of taking action*

Time-out to practise

Continue to reflect on a time when something did not go according to plan.

1. What moods or emotions were present?
2. How did those moods and emotions help or hinder you?
3. What moods and emotions may have been more useful for you?

Body

Our body plays a key role in our Way of Being, yet we often overlook the body as an influencer of our actions and behaviours.

Olalla (2004) notes we have forgotten how to use our bodies as a guide for our health and wellbeing and that we have also lost the ability to understand how our body and emotions relate. Olalla further claims we are unaware of how our physical health depends on the stories we tell ourselves to make meaning of the world. He suggests a link between illness, our social and personal stories, and the emotions we connect to them.

In *Your Body is Your Brain: Leverage your somatic intelligence to find purpose, build resilience, deepen relationships and lead more powerfully*, Amanda Blake (2018) refers to our body as our 'social and emotional sense organ'. Everything within us is housed by our body, and all actions come from our body. When we notice what is happening in our body, we can understand how this influences our actions.

How can our body affect our Way of Being? Table 4 shows actions we might take from different body configurations. The actions listed are examples only. They are not representative of how things must be; they are merely examples of how things *might* be. Different actions may be available to you. The important point is to notice how our body influences our actions.

Request: 'Would you change my tyre, please?'	
Body	**What action is most likely?**
• Diminished, heavy, shallow breathing with sighing, concave chest	• Do nothing; can't be bothered.
• Flushed, heavy, shallow, weak breathing, head down, shoulders slumped, concave chest	• Avoid making the request, perhaps not wanting others to be aware of what happened.
• Full body, open to others, head held high, ready to move on and see what is waiting for us	• Make the request, being curious about what might happen.

Table 4: *Our body plays a key role in our actions and outcomes*

Time-out to practise

Again, continue reflecting on a time when something did not go according to plan.

1. What was happening within your body?
2. What was your breathing like?
3. What sensations did you notice throughout your body?
4. How did your body help or not help you take action?

A shift in our Way of Being

Our Way of Being will either support us in taking useful action or not support us. Because we don't always see the choices we are making, we aren't always aware of how our Way of Being is serving us. If we aren't aware of when our Way of Being is serving or not serving us, we won't understand when or how to shift it.

Alex and Maggie discussed the process that would be followed during their conversations. This process can be used whenever we want to shift our Way of Being to bring about different actions. The steps in the process are as follows:

1. Declare that there is an issue.
2. Seek to understand the issue.
3. Explore possible ways forward.
4. Declare a way forward.
5. Take action.
6. Reflect on the results.

This process is discussed in detail in Chapter 11. However, the objective of the model is to determine the Way of Being that sits behind our challenge, explore how those ways of being may be contributing to the challenge, and then explore and declare new ways of being to support future action. By understanding the Way of Being and how our learning informs it, we can choose a useful Way of Being for achieving the intended results.

It is important to note that each Way of Being is legitimate for where we are in life at any point in time. Operating from a Way of Being that isn't serving us isn't wrong. Rather, a new Way of Being may enable more useful action, helping us to bring about whatever we want to create in life.

You might be wondering what role past learning plays in shifting our Way of Being. Let's look at this more closely. Our Way of Being comes from our prior learning about interacting in life. If our learning is no longer serving us, that doesn't mean we are without knowledge or that our learning was wrong. It simply means we will benefit from new ways of being and doing.

Imagine playing the three notes b, a, and g on the piano. As the only notes in *Hot Cross Buns*, these notes are useful if *Hot Cross Buns* is the song we want to play. However, if we want to play Mozart's *Piano Concerto No. 21*, the notes b, a, and g alone are not useful. This doesn't mean our learning was wrong if those were the only notes we learnt to play as a child. Knowing those musical notes was useful in the past, and that knowledge might continue to serve us in the future. However, to shift to a future where playing Mozart is possible, we will need to expand our learning.

Like learning a new song on the piano, sometimes our learning in terms of how to interact with others needs an update. This is because as life changes, our old learning becomes less useful. For example, we may work well with our current manager. However, when a new manager arrives with different priorities, focus and values, how we interacted with the previous manager may not work as well. We are in a new situation that requires a new Way of Being. By expanding our learning, we can create a new Way of Being to help us interact with the new manager.

The key to begin shifting our Way of Being is to notice it. In Step 2 of the process that Alex described to Maggie, we seek to understand the issue by drawing our attention to the Way of Being behind it. The idea is to become aware of the Way of Being that is informing our behaviours within the issue. This is best done from a place of curiosity, perhaps starting with the following self-reflection questions:

- What am I saying to myself about this situation and the people involved?
- How are the moods and emotions I have attached to this situation helping or not helping me and the people involved?
- What am I noticing in my body—sensations, breathing, tension, posture?
- How are my language, moods and emotions, and body serving me?

When we understand how our Way of Being is serving (or not serving) us, we can identify future actions.

Time-out to practise

Reflect once again on the situation where things did not go according to plan:

1. What new Way of Being might be useful in this situation?
2. What is missing for you to shift to this new Way of Being?

A Deeper Reflection

Find a quiet place to pause and focus on your current Way of Being.

1. What are you saying to yourself about yourself?
2. What are you saying to yourself about others?
3. What are you saying to yourself about your current situation?
4. What moods and emotions are present?
5. What do you notice about your posture?
6. What do you notice about your breathing?
7. What sensations are you noticing within your body?
8. How is your current Way of Being serving or not serving you?
9. What might be useful for you to shift in your current Way of Being?
10. How will you shift your Way of Being?
11. What was happening to you as a learner while you were progressing through this chapter?

Key Points

- Humans are a product of our history and the rules we learn throughout our lives.
- We can shift our rules.
- Our Way of Being is the interrelationship between our language, moods and emotions, and body.
- We see the world from our Way of Being.
- Our language comprises how we speak, think, listen and form interpretations.
- Moods and emotions are always with us. Our body is home to everything we do and plays an essential role in our Way of Being.
- We can shift our Way of Being to generate more useful actions.

CHAPTER 5

How do I stop worrying and start taking action?

The Story

Alex and Maggie sat in Alex's home office, ready to talk about Maggie's work challenges.

Alex is about to find out how incompetent I am. I am going to look like an idiot. Let's hope we can do this without him deciding I am a lost cause.

Alex spoke first.

'You said doubt and low self-esteem stop you from doing your job. Can you elaborate?'

Silence.

Gosh, time to open up…

'Confidence has always been a struggle for me, although I survive by faking it. In the past, I worked hard to understand the ins and outs of my job and find things I am good at. This strategy has helped me to be confident and handle whatever comes up. I may not always have every answer, but I somehow manage to get through.'

'How is this approach helping you now?'

My approach is not helping me at all. That's why I am here.

'To be honest, the approach isn't helping. This job is too big, and I can't know everything. My background knowledge doesn't support my decision-making in this role. I used to put strategies in place to help me fake being confident. Now, I can't fake it anymore. I am unsure of how to do anything in this new job. People expect me to make decisions, but I can't because they aren't giving me the backstories. I feel like my hands are tied because I don't understand the environment. I am frozen because I am so unsure of what to do.'

'You've mentioned "faking it" a few times. Can you explain what you mean by that?'

I didn't expect Alex's questions to be so hard.

After a pause, Maggie responded, 'I guess it means appearing on top of my game and being able to find a plan, even though I may not have all the answers. Having the possibility of being in control. Right now, everything is a struggle.'

'What do you mean by "struggle"?'

Everything is hard work. Outcomes are difficult to achieve.

Maggie hesitated while finding her words.

'Nothing is easy for me to achieve.'

Alex waited for Maggie to continue.

Oh, my goodness. Silence. Alex is waiting for me to say more.

'I struggle because I worry about doing the wrong thing. If I can't work out how to do the right thing, I don't cope. I am not safe when I know I might make a mistake.'

'So, you must always be right? Is that what you are saying?'

*No, it's not quite what I mean. But what **do** I mean?*

Alex waited.

'What I mean is, I must do things the right way. I don't care about *being* right, but I must always *do* the right thing.'

'What is the difference between being right and doing the right thing?'

Maggie stared out the window. Alex didn't hurry the silence, allowing her all the time she needed.

Alex's garden is so lovely. Perhaps if I focus on the garden, I won't need to make eye contact when I am struggling to answer his questions.

'Being right means knowing the right answer. If you asked me a question, being right would mean giving you a correct answer. Being wrong would mean giving you an incorrect answer.'

Alex persisted, 'How is *being* right different from *doing* the right thing?'

'Doing the right thing is more about my decisions. My managers have asked me to come up with a plan for my team's direction. I don't have the history or a clear understanding of my role. So, how do I decide? If I make the wrong decision, I will let my team, my managers and the organisation down.'

Now Alex will realise I am incompetent.

'Why does making the wrong decision matter?'

'I must make choices I can stand by, and I don't want to be judged for making the wrong decision.'

'Does a right or wrong answer exist?'

What does Alex mean? Of course, my choices can be right or wrong. If my decision is wrong, we will fail.

'Well, the team might fail if I make the wrong decision.'

'What is the right answer and what is the wrong answer?'

Here is my problem. I have no answers, right or wrong!

As Maggie studied every detail of the garden, the silence grew.

I don't have an answer. Why can't I come up with an answer? I am so dumb.

Alex said, 'Can I offer a suggestion?'

'Sure.'

He might as well. I've got nothing.

'Perhaps there isn't a right answer. Perhaps there is only a best answer.'

'What do you mean?'

'Can I share some observations with you?'

'Sure.'

'I heard you say that you don't mind being wrong. So, if I asked you a question and you gave me the wrong answer, you wouldn't mind? You could accept you did not provide the known right answer?'

'Yes, that's right.'

'Then I heard you say that doing the right thing is more about making the right decisions. However, you don't know what decision would be the right one to make. At the same time, you don't want to do the wrong thing.'

'Yes.'

'Could "doing the right thing" be about making a choice when the answer isn't clear? Perhaps, unlike "getting things right", there is no one right answer, and so the answer you are looking for doesn't exist. Could you perhaps be looking for the answer that best fits the situation based on the information available to you?'

'I guess so.'

'What if you let go of what is right and wrong and simply did your best?'

Alex waited for Maggie to speak. She focused on the garden.

But how can I choose the best answer when I don't understand the information available to me?

'I understand what you are saying, Alex. The answers may not be right or wrong for the decisions I am being asked to make at work. Perhaps I should just find the *best* answer. But even that is overwhelming because what is the "best fit" answer?'

'Can you name the emotion you are experiencing when you are trying to decide?'

Alex waited.

'Gosh, I'm struggling to think of the emotion I feel at those times. I just feel uncertain when there are so many unknowns.'

'So, uncertainty?'

'Yes.'

Alex waited, allowing the silence to speak.

Maggie broke the silence first. 'The thing is, I am unsure how to process the information available to me to find the best answer.'

Alex paused before continuing. 'Maggie, would you be open to exploring what is happening in your body when you are uncertain?'

This is weird!

'What do you mean?'

'Our body can give us useful cues about our Way of Being. It can provide learning that may not be otherwise accessible. Areas to look into can include our posture, breathing, body sensations, how we are using parts of our body, and areas of tension. We house our language, moods and emotions in our body so our body can provide clues about our Way of Being. I suggest we role-play it so you can see what I mean.'

'Sounds different, but I'm open to giving it a try.'

'Are you certain? All of my suggestions are an invitation. You can say no if you want to.'

'I'm sure.'

'Okay, let's stand up for this one. Please choose a spot anywhere in the room to stand.'

Maggie stood near the window.

I hope this body thing isn't too weird.

'I invite you to remember a time when you faced one of those uncertain work situations you described.'

Maggie closed her eyes as she visualised a previous conversation with one of her senior managers.

Alex continued, 'What are you saying to yourself about the uncertainty?'

'I must become certain so I don't do the wrong thing.'

'And what are you saying to the uncertainty?'

'I want the uncertainty to go away.'

'So, you are telling the uncertainty to go away?'

'Yes, uncertainty shouldn't be there.'

'Can you describe what is happening in your body?'

'I am unsure. Could you be more specific, please?'

'Sure. I am curious about how your body is when you are telling the uncertainty to go away. What do you notice about your posture? Or your breathing? What sensations are present? Is there any tension? Draw your attention to what is happening in your body.'

I am not sure how this will help, but sure...

Alex waited as Maggie focused on her body.

'My body has shrunk. I am stuck. I am not in control.'

'Anything else?'

'I feel kind of ... out of balance. My breathing is faster and not as deep. I've got butterflies in the pit of my stomach. I don't like the way I'm feeling. It's making me uncomfortable.'

'Stop if you would like to remove the discomfort.'

Maggie stopped and opened her eyes.

I feel so heavy and full of worry.

Alex said, 'Try shaking and wriggling your body to remove the discomfort.'

Wow, shaking and moving helped. Weird.

Alex gave Maggie some time to regroup before speaking. 'I would like to invite you to find a new spot to stand in, so you can remove yourself from the uncomfortable feeling.'

Maggie chose a new spot, still in front of the window.

'Gosh, I am drained after paying attention to my body.'

'Yes, sometimes working with the body can be intense. However, the body can also help us learn. Would you like to share some of your experience?'

The sun reflected off a photo frame on Alex's desk, distracting Maggie for a few seconds.

'I found the question about what I was saying to the uncertainty interesting.'

Alex asked, 'In what way?'

'Well, I realised I try to make the uncertainty go away. I don't want uncertainty around.'

'Why?'

'Because I find uncertainty confronting. I can't handle being uncertain, so I want it to go away.'

'Great! Would you mind if I offered something?'

> *Alex always asks my permission before suggesting things. I'm not sure why. Lord knows I need all the help I can get.*

'Sure.'

'You mentioned you wanted uncertainty to go away. One view is that when we oppose uncertainty, as though we are trying to push it out of the way, we create anxiety. I am wondering if this resonates at all?'

'Anxiety?'

'Yes. It may not be relevant for you.'

> *Wow. Anxiety. Well, I worry when I am uncertain. I never considered it as being anxiety, though.*

'What do you mean when you say "anxiety"?'

'When we operate from anxiety, we worry. It's like we fear something but are unsure of what we fear. We try to protect ourselves, aiming our actions at self-protection. I am not talking about a diagnosed anxiety disorder, but those moments where we may feel anxious.'

Maggie stared at the window, trying to find her words. This time she paid no attention to the garden, her search for understanding was too deep.

'I never considered myself an anxious person. But I take your point. I don't want there to be uncertainty, so I am trying to push it away. And I am worrying a lot. Wow.'

Alex and Maggie sat in silence until Maggie spoke again.

'So, what do we do now?'

'Well, what is the opposite of pushing uncertainty away?'

'Welcoming it?'

'Yes. Or, at least, accepting that uncertainty is present.'

How?

'How do I accept uncertainty?'

'Would you be open to exploring the body again?'

As weird as this sounds, bodywork helped last time, so why not?

'Yes, that would be useful.'

'Fantastic. Let's start by finding another spot to stand.'

Maggie stood near the bookcase. She closed her eyes, listening for Alex's cues.

'Can you recall a time when you were uncertain, yet you were also comfortable with the uncertainty?'

Maggie paused for some time.

'A friend and I went hiking with her children. We took a wrong turn and lost our way. But I knew we were never in any real danger because we could retrace our steps.'

'What did you do to accept the uncertainty?'

'We turned the experience into a game. My friend's children are young, so we played "Where did we walk last?" with them. We turned back and asked the children whether they remembered significant landmarks from our walk. We asked them to help us find the landmarks as we walked. When we found a landmark, we celebrated. In the end, we found the path and enjoyed our walk.'

'Tell me what was happening within you as you played the game?'

'I enjoyed the game. As we walked, I wondered what landmarks the children would remember.'

'Can you embrace the moment and experience how it occurred in your body?'

Maggie paused, trying to embody her experience of the hike.

'I didn't worry about missing the path. I wanted to keep playing the game and exploring. When I imagine our experience, my body is more upright and open. I want to open my eyes and take in what is happening around me. I am absorbed in the moment, wanting to keep exploring and finding new things. There is a tingling sensation in my torso. I don't mind what happens because I want to explore. I am not worried. My chest is open. I want to take deep breaths and absorb everything.'

> *Oh my gosh, I became so focused on imagining the walk, I ended up opening my eyes without realising. Cool! Although, how will a past hike help me with anxiety?*

'How did you find that activity?'

'Amazing!'

'Would you be open to trying one more thing?'

'Yes, let's go.'

'Let's take a couple of steps to the right so we are away from where you discovered anxiety. When you are ready, I invite you to take a moment to find your work body, where you are opposing uncertainty.'

It only took a few seconds for Maggie to visualise her experience of work.

'What would you move from this place to how you were feeling on the hike? What did you do on the hike that might be helpful for you to do here?'

A pause.

'I paid attention to my surroundings. I wanted to take everything in.'

'Excellent. Would lifting your head and shoulders be helpful?'

Maggie inhaled, eyes shut.

'There is a slight difference. When I lift my head and shoulders, my body draws up, and I don't want to miss out on anything. I want to take everything in.'

'And what about your breathing?'

'My breathing is slowing down and becoming deeper.'

'And what is that like?'

'I am still a little worried about the uncertainty. Not as much, but some stories are still present.'

'What's the dominant story that comes to mind?'

'What if I am not good enough?'

'How can you change your story to one like the story you told yourself on your hike?'

Another deep breath as Maggie reflected on what might help her.

No idea.

'I am unsure how to change my story. Any suggestions?'

'Well, I wonder whether it would be useful to ask yourself, "What if I *am* good enough?"'

I like it.

'Perhaps.'

'What would help you to change that story?'

Maggie took a deep breath, deeply noticing what was happening within her before speaking.

'As I lift my shoulders to look around, if I pause to take a deep breath and open my torso, it seems easier to say to myself, "What if I *am* good enough?" It almost feels natural.'

'Great! Would you like to try making the shift again, or do you think it might be too uncomfortable?'

'I would like to try again.'

'Would you like me to help by talking you through the process, or do you want to try without my guidance?'

'I would like to try on my own.'

> *Wow. I never expected to be trying anything on my own. This stuff is weird, but it is also quite amazing.*

'Excellent. Perhaps you can talk me through the process?'

Maggie closed her eyes as she imagined pushing away uncertainty.

'I can sense anxiety throughout my body, and I am aware of the position of my shoulders and head. Being aware of those things is useful because I know I can change my posture to create a body that is more likely to support my declaration.'

'Excellent.'

Maggie inhaled, lifting her shoulders up and back and raising her head.

As she exhaled, she asked herself aloud, 'What if I *am* good enough?'

'How was that?' asked Alex.

'Helpful. When I noticed uncertainty being pushed away, taking a deep breath helped me move to acceptance. Lifting my shoulders up and back felt natural and helped me lift my head and pay attention to everything around me. The change in my posture supported me to accept the uncertainty and see it as less daunting.'

'Great! Would you like to shake off any left-over emotions and sit down?'

'Sure.'

They sat in their seats.

Alex asked, 'So, what moods and emotions appeared when you explored the different states of your body?'

'Anxiety at first. Then, when I shifted to the new body, I wanted to explore the world around me and find out more. I'm not sure how to label the new emotion, but I said, "I wonder..." to myself a lot.'

'I wonder what emotions help us explore and find out more?'

Maggie paused before responding hesitantly.

'Could it be curiosity?'

'Yes, curiosity sounds fitting.'

'I am not sure what else.'

'Can I share something with you?'

Please do. I am making this up as I go, and I appreciate the insights.

'Sure.'

'We spoke of opposing uncertainty or pushing it away. We can also accept uncertainty, which helps create wonder or curiosity. Perhaps this is what you did during the hike?'

'Ah, yes. I agree.'

'So, how will this help with your work situation?'

'I found it helpful to identify that I was experiencing anxiety. Until then, everything felt crazy and out of control. However, naming what I felt gave me an understanding of what I was dealing with. I now have ideas for using my body to shift from anxiety to curiosity, which is useful.'

Look at me, talking about shifting anxiety by shifting my body! It's a good thing Alex never mentioned bodywork during our first phone call. I would have ended the call straight away!

'And how will you shift from anxiety to curiosity at work?' Alex continued.

'I now understand how anxiety occurs in my body. From now on, whenever I am anxious, I will pause, take a deep breath, and lift my shoulders and head. I can also check what I am saying to myself and try to become curious. Being curious will enable me to handle the situation in a more useful way.'

'Is that achievable?'

'Yes.'

'How does this relate back to your original story of always having to do the right thing?'

Alex misses nothing!

'I guess not knowing how to choose made the story unhelpful for me. And the uncertainty made me uncomfortable. If I am more at peace with uncertainty, the story becomes less relevant. Also, I won't always know the best choice until after the event. So maybe I can shift my story to something like, "I wonder what the best choice is, given the information I have available?" Perhaps this is about accepting uncertainty and shifting to a new story with less pressure.'

'Are you able to do that?'

'Yes. I will need some practice, but I can do this.'

'So where are we at?'

'I am comfortable that what I have learnt will shift how I am being at work, which is more than I had hoped for today. So, I am okay with stopping if you are happy to.'

'Fabulous. Before we finish, it's useful to declare a new way forward. What declaration would you like to make, Maggie?'

She remained silent before asking, 'How do I make a declaration?'

'One way is to think about how you want to be and then declare it as though you have already achieved your goal. For example, "I am a curious leader of people," or something relevant to you.'

Ah, I understand.

Maggie took a few minutes to consider what she would declare.

I am amazed that Alex stays silent for as long as I do, and it's not at all awkward.

'My declaration is, "I am a curious person, in wonder about what I can create and achieve. I may get things wrong, and that is okay."'

I didn't realise I could be so wise. This is exciting!

'Wow. Well done.'

'Thank you, Alex.'

I just paid someone to tell me to lift my shoulders and head and wonder about what I can achieve. People will think I am mad if I tell them. Yet, the conversation helped. I don't fully understand this Way of Being idea yet, but it's shaping up to be useful so far.

The Learning

Our stories

As Maggie is discovering, our stories can help us or limit us. Her story of 'I must do the right thing' affects her actions and choices. It is creating uncertainty because she isn't sure *how* to get things right, leading her to suffer in her role as she feels unable to take action. Our stories can impact any aspect of our lives. Sometimes, the suffering might be like a bump in the road. Other times, it can be debilitating.

Human beings create stories to help give meaning to our experiences. As 'meaning factories', we take information into our body via various senses. We then compare this data to our prior learning, which helps us produce meaning through stories. Our Way of Being is the place from which we see the world. It informs our interpretation and the meaning we create. We might create an alternative meaning each time we view the same situation from a different Way of Being.

Let's look at an example. A colleague arrives late for a meeting. The information the world is giving us is that the colleague is late. However, we will apply our own past learning about meetings, time management, ourselves, this colleague and others to make meaning of the colleague being late. Examples of the meaning we might create are:

- The colleague is disrespectful of people's time.
- The colleague is inconsiderate towards others.
- The colleague is busy and needs our help.
- The colleague was late.
- The colleague is always late to meetings organised by a particular person.
- The colleague has challenges in their personal life, so we should be kind.

Each of us can create a different meaning from the information the world is giving us. One person might label a colleague who is late for a meeting as disrespectful, while another might assess the colleague as requiring support. We each create different meanings depending on how we view the world from our current Way of Being. In other words, our Way of Being in each moment informs the meaning we create about a matter, event or situation.

We create stories to help us understand our place in the world through how we listen, form opinions and interpret the world. Our stories rely on our Way of Being, yet they also contribute to it. Furthermore, the meaning we create influences our interactions with ourselves and others.

In *Stories We Tell Ourselves: Making Meaning in a Meaningless Universe,* Richard Holloway (2020) suggests the stories we live by provide our rules for living life. This implies that our stories underpin who we are and provide rules for our actions. In Chapter 4, Maggie and Alex discussed Maggie's learning of manners. If the story we live by is 'Good people are well-mannered', this creates rules for how we live. The rules will depend on our personal interpretation of manners. Examples might be:

- We must always use good manners.
- It is wrong not to use good manners.
- We must always say please, thank you, sorry, hello and goodbye.
- We must always take our hat off indoors.
- Manners are outdated.
- People will understand that I meant to imply please or thank you.
- We must always respect the elderly, regardless of their behaviour.

Our rules will specify how we act in life and how we view the actions of others. We may form moral judgements about people and how we want to interact with them based on how we apply these rules. Often, we won't realise we are using our rules to form judgements. Our rules can be so invisible that we may not be aware of their existence.

When we create stories and rules, we also create and remove boundaries for how we interact in life. For something to be true, something else becomes not true. This is how we create boundaries. For example, if we believe it true that a good person must always be well-mannered, then it is not true that a good person is never well-mannered. Regardless of whether we mean to, our rule has created a boundary between what we consider as good and bad people from the perspective of manners. Other life rules also create boundaries, often without us realising.

Our rules and stories define our actions. Maggie found her stories and rules disallow 'doing the wrong thing'. Her rules tell her she must do the right thing, yet her experience of the world challenges her ability to live by her rules. The gap between her rules and experience has led Maggie to judge herself and push uncertainty away. In other words, she assessed the situation as uncertain, meaning she could not confidently know or predict what would happen, and then reacted by opposing the uncertainty, figuratively pushing it away.

We may not realise it, but our stories are silent declarations of how we exist in the world. When we are aware of what our stories are declaring for us, we can consider shifting to a Way of Being that allows us to make different declarations. Maggie did this when she shifted from having to get things right to being curious about what would happen.

So how do we shift our stories? The key is to start by acknowledging and understanding what stories exist. Ask yourself:

- What am I telling myself about this situation?
- What moods and emotions have I attached to these stories?
- How am I holding my stories (language), moods and emotions in my body?
- What permission do I need to give myself to change my story?

As humans, we are in a constant cycle of making sense of our world. Stories are essential to this process. Our stories can help us grow. But they can also limit us, highlighting the importance of understanding them and why they exist.

Time-out to practise

Take a moment to pause and listen to the stories you are telling yourself right now.

1. What stories are you hearing?
2. How are these stories helping you?
3. How are these stories limiting you?
4. How might changing the stories be helpful?

The difference between moods and emotions

As we navigate life, we experience emotions. For example, when we lose a loved one, we experience sadness. When we break a personal standard, we experience guilt. If we assess something to be morally wrong, we experience anger.

Emotions incline us towards a specific action. Sadness inclines us to mourn the loss of what we deem as important to us. Guilt inclines us to punish ourselves. Anger inclines us to punish the source of the injustice or wrongdoing. In each case, the emotion serves a purpose.

Moods, on the other hand, are a more over-arching approach to life. They are longer-lasting and are often invisible to us. They provide a lens for viewing life, often without us realising we are looking through a lens.

As Maggie and Alex talked, Maggie determined she was facing uncertainty in her daily work. When we assess something as uncertain, we say that we can't confidently predict what will happen. Uncertainty is normal and even necessary. When we visit a busy shopping centre, we may be uncertain about whether we will find a parking spot. When starting a new job, we may be uncertain about what others expect of us. Uncertainty can help us prepare. However, sometimes, it can get in the way.

Sieler (2007) suggests we can respond to uncertainty in one of two ways:

1. We can push uncertainty away (opposing uncertainty), or
2. We can be comfortable with uncertainty (accepting uncertainty).

As Figure 7 shows, Sieler (2007) proposes that we create anxiety when we push uncertainty away. He describes anxiety as '[...] a strong desire for the certainty of a non-threatening future' (p. 267) and claims we focus on self-protection when anxious. His description makes sense if we consider that anxiety is about wanting to remove a threat. It is also consistent with Maggie's behaviour, where she is trying to remove the threat of getting things wrong. Her focus is on herself and what is happening to her. She is worried about the threat that the uncertainty is creating. She may want to focus on others around her, yet anxiety makes this a challenge because it leads her to focus on self-protection.

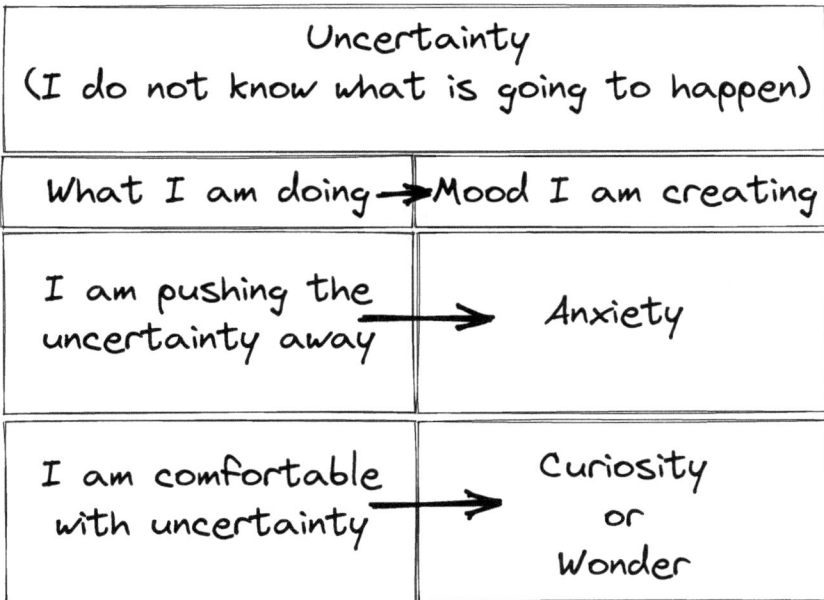

Uncertainty (I do not know what is going to happen)	
What I am doing →	Mood I am creating
I am pushing the uncertainty away →	Anxiety
I am comfortable with uncertainty →	Curiosity or Wonder

Figure 7: *Moods we can create from uncertainty*

Sieler (2007) proposes we create the mood of wonder when we accept uncertainty. In Figure 7, we interpret this as wonder or curiosity. In this mood, we focus on the wonders the world offers, ignoring uncertainty as a threat. Unlike anxiety, in wonder, we don't find it necessary to self-protect, and our focus is on what is happening in the world.

Alex helps Maggie shift to a mood of wonder, altering her interpretation that uncertainty will harm her. Maggie demonstrates this shift in her declaration: 'I am a curious person, in wonder about what I can create and achieve. I may get things wrong, and that is ok.'

In developing awareness of our moods and how we are being in life, we remember that whatever is happening in our language, moods and emotions, and body is valid. Our aim is not to judge but to accept ourselves as legitimate. When we decide to shift a mood, we are not labelling the original mood as wrong. Rather, shifting a mood enables us to move to a place where we can take more useful action. In doing so, we create new possibilities for interacting with ourselves and others. This does not make our previous actions wrong. It might simply show that those actions were not serving us in a useful way.

Time-out to practise

1. Where are you noticing uncertainty in your life?
2. How are you responding to the uncertainty?
3. If you are pushing the uncertainty away, what would help you accept it?
4. If you are comfortable with the uncertainty, what can you learn from this that would help you deal with uncertainty in the future?

Our body is home to our language, moods and emotions

When our Way of Being is not serving us, it is worth observing what is happening in our body. Doing so can help us understand our language, moods and emotions, which reside in the body. So, what can our body tell us?

Each story we tell ourselves and each mood or emotion we experience causes our body to react. Our reactions are not always obvious to us. We might just feel 'a bit off', 'bad' or 'good', and so on. However, when we draw our attention to how our body is responding, we can learn more about our language, moods and emotions and how to shift them.

Figure 8 shows one experience of the emotion of sadness to highlight an example of the learning our body can make available to us. Without awareness of these feelings, we may not understand our experience of sadness. As we notice each bodily experience, we can gain an understanding of why they exist and what they are telling us. With sadness, perhaps we notice that our body is telling us it wants some time out to come to terms with what we have lost. Maybe the lack of 'sparkle' is telling us that what we have lost is important to us.

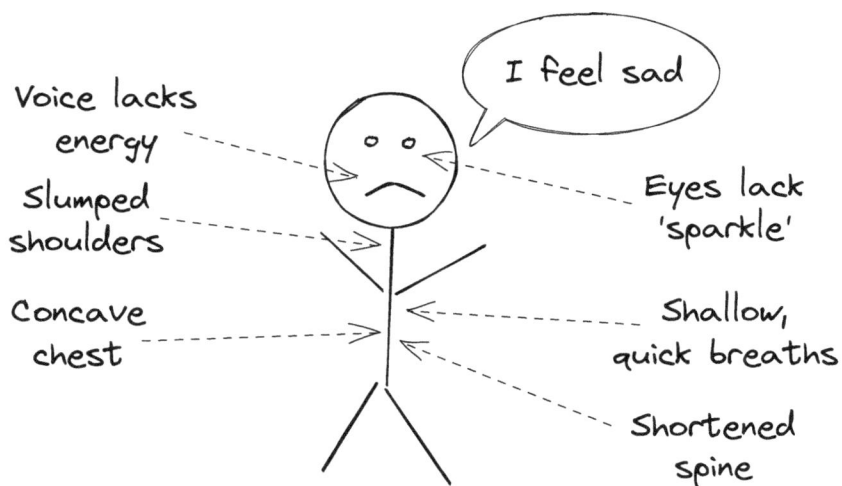

Voice lacks energy

Slumped shoulders

Concave chest

I feel sad

Eyes lack 'sparkle'

Shallow, quick breaths

Shortened spine

Figure 8: *Our body gives us information about how we are experiencing life*

When we understand what sadness is telling us, we can choose what we want to do with it. Possible actions could include:

- sitting with the sadness to remember what we have lost, or
- finding something else to focus on that creates a different emotion, or
- choosing a different action from what we might be inclined to take, such as having a conversation.

The point is that with awareness we have choice.

When we explore our Way of Being in our body, we can learn to identify signs that a particular emotion is present. When we understand these signs, we can also learn why the emotion is present and how we can shift our body to bring about different moods and emotions if that would be useful.

As an example of using our body's sensations as signs of the moods and emotions present and how to shift them, let me share my experience of anxiety. When I am anxious, I experience a sensation at the bottom of my stomach. Some might describe this as butterflies. To me, grasshoppers is a more apt description! When this sensation is present for me, anxiety is present. It is my signal to pause, lift my shoulders up and back, open my torso and slow my breathing. This works for me in noticing and shifting my anxiety. Your experience may vary from this. You may notice signs I don't. Alternatively, the signs you notice may differ from my experience. This is expected since we are each interpreting ourselves and life differently.

Time-out to practise

1. What sensations, posture and breathing are present in your body at the moment?
2. What are they telling you about how you are interpreting the world?

A Deeper Reflection

Choose a situation that isn't going as you would like it to.

1. What are you labelling as uncertain in this situation?
2. What are you telling yourself about accepting uncertainty?
3. Where does uncertainty sit in your body?
4. What moods or emotions might help you?
5. How could you shift your body to create these new moods and emotions?
6. What will you do differently in this situation?
7. What was happening for you as a learner while you were progressing through this chapter?

Key Points

- As humans, we use stories to help us make sense of the world. We are 'meaning-making factories'.
- Our stories can become the rules by which we live.
- Our stories and rules can help us or limit us.
- Emotions are a response to specific circumstances. They are usually short-lived.
- Moods are overarching lenses for how we see the world and can last from an hour to a lifetime.
- We embody our stories, moods and emotions.
- When we are aware of our stories and rules and the moods and emotions we attach to them, we can effect change in ourselves.

CHAPTER 6

Why do I doubt myself?

The Story

Maggie arrived for her third session with Alex. He greeted her warmly at the door.

As they sat down, Alex asked, 'So, what has been happening since we last met?'

'Well, I have found ways of dealing with my anxiety. I mean, I'm not perfect, but at least I can now recognise anxiety and try to do something useful when it appears.'

'Fabulous!'

'Yes, agreed. Let me give you an example. I met with a manager who can be quite aggressive in meetings. Normally, I would put my head down, avoid eye contact, and slink into my chair. However, I took a deep breath and opened my torso, just as we had practised. Although I experienced some anxiety, I was ready to deal with the meeting.'

'Well done! Anything else you would like to share before we kick off today's conversation?'

'I struggled to remember to pay attention to my Way of Being. So, I set a reminder on my phone for every two and a half hours throughout the day. When the alarm sounded, I took two to three minutes to check in on what I was saying to myself, the moods and emotions I was experiencing, and how my body was responding. That was useful. I learnt quite a lot by paying attention to what was happening in my Way of Being.'

'That's great, Maggie!'

'Thank you. This approach really made a difference.'

'So...what would you like to discuss today?'

'Today, I want to talk about doubt, particularly at work.'

'Sure. Can you tell me more? What are you experiencing?'

Maggie looked out the window towards the garden, her favourite place to look when she wanted to pull her thoughts together. She remained silent for some time. Alex waited in silence until she was ready to speak.

'Well, I worry less about getting things right. I mean, I still worry. However, I am learning how to navigate my story about getting things right. But I still doubt myself a lot. I start something, but I don't believe I can do it. I question myself, and I freeze. Doubt holds me back. It stops me from getting my work done. I want things to be different.'

'What do you believe you can't do?'

'To be honest, most of my job. It's like I don't trust myself.'

'Tell me more about not trusting yourself. What do you mean?'

Oh gosh, my eyes are welling up. Don't cry, Maggie. Hold it together.

The cockatoos in the garden were making a noise.

Take a deep breath. You can do this.

Somehow, Maggie kept her tears at bay.

'I don't trust myself to do my job because I am not capable.'

'So, is trust about your perceived level of competence? Or something else?'

Perceived. Nice touch, Alex.

'Yes. I believe I am not competent. The job is unfamiliar, and I am unsure how to proceed.'

'Would you trust yourself in your job if you believed you had the skills?'

'Yes.'

'So, what do you trust yourself to do at work?'

'What do you mean?'

'There must be things you trust yourself to do. What are they?'

I have no idea.

'I'm sorry. I am stuck. I don't know how to answer that question. I don't trust myself to do much at work.'

'There is no need to apologise, Maggie.'

Alex is silent again. I have to say something. What will I say? I have to fill the silence! There must be something. I mean, all I can think of is I trust myself to be decent towards others. Maybe I will just go with that.

'I trust myself to treat people with respect.'

'That's a great start. What else?'

Wasn't one answer enough?

'I trust myself to help my team when they are stuck.'

'Tell me more. Do you have an example?'

'Last week, a team member came to me, quite upset about something. They didn't know what to do. I listened and helped find a resolution.'

'What actions did you take?'

'Well, I knew there were some formal processes I would need to follow to help support this person. I had no idea what those processes were in my current workplace. However, it is my job to support my staff, so I knew I had to find a way forward.'

'What did you do?'

'I paused and asked myself what I would do next. I had a rough idea, but not specific to our organisation. I was confident I could work it out if I asked the right people.'

'It sounds to me as though you didn't really trust yourself to follow the organisation's procedures without help. Is that fair, or am I off track?'

'I guess it's fair. I mean, I *am* new, so how would I know until I need to use them?'

'Agreed. What was interesting for me was you seemed to trust yourself to work out what to do. I could be wrong, but that's what it sounded like.'

Wow. That's pretty cool.

'Gosh, I never even realised. Yes, I did trust myself to work things out.'

'So, you mentioned you don't assess yourself as competent in your current job. Where do you trust yourself to work things out?'

'Can I reflect on that for a moment, please?'

'Of course.'

The cockatoos have gone. Gee, they made a mess in the garden.

'I have realised I can usually work most things out. I either ask for help or assess the situation and come up with a plan. I won't always do it straight away, and I may need time. But I know there are always ways to move forward. I trust myself to work things out, at least most of the time.'

'When don't you trust yourself to work things out?'

'When someone has thrown me something with no context, no background information and a short time to decide my approach. I feel overwhelmed and don't think to break the task down.'

'Ah.'

'Whenever I am unsure about something, I become caught in a cycle of being unable to complete a task. And I don't trust myself when I am unsure. What if I trusted myself to work it out? That way, instead of focusing on the task, I could focus on working it out.'

'How would that help?'

'It would shift my focus and help me see things differently. I would still be unsure of how to proceed, but I would trust myself to work out my next steps. It would be incredibly helpful.'

'Great! Now, imagine you are at that point now, of trusting yourself to work out your next steps. Tell me where you're at now?'

'I have a way forward. And I'm looking forward to seeing how I will work things out. However, doubt is still lurking.'

'If you could chat with doubt, what would it be saying to you?'

Maggie's eyebrows raised.

Probably one of your weirdest questions yet, Alex.

It was some time before Maggie responded.

'Doubt would say, "Maggie, you are unsure."'

'Unsure of what?'

'Unsure of how to proceed.'

'Okay. Great. And if you were to assume that doubt's only role was to give you a message and not judge you, why would doubt give you that specific message? Remember, doubt is a friend with a message, not a judge.'

A friend? Seriously?

Another pause.

'Perhaps doubt is telling me I am unsure and to be careful.'

'How is it helpful to be receiving that message?'

'Viewing it as a message and not a judgement is quite freeing. I am grateful for being given the message. It is helping me to see what is happening.'

'Fantastic! So, what actions do you think doubt inclines you towards?'

'I seem to hesitate.'

'Excellent. How does hesitating help you when you are uncertain of how to proceed?'

'I'm not sure. Would hesitation be protecting me?'

'It could be. I also have another interpretation. Do I have your permission to offer it?'

Thank goodness!

'Yes. I would appreciate that.'

'What if doubt *wanted* you to hesitate? When we hesitate, we buy time. What if doubt was giving you time to plan?'

'I like that explanation. Doubt becomes about creating a plan rather than not being good enough.'

'We often see emotions as a judgement of who we are. This isn't always a useful interpretation. Emotions offer messages about how we are seeing life. It's not right or wrong to experience doubt. You wouldn't know you were unsure if doubt didn't appear, so it is being helpful.'

'That's an interesting approach to emotions.'

'Is it useful for you?'

'Yes.'

'So, Maggie, if doubt is giving you time to plan, would it be helpful to accept it and welcome it as a friend?'

You want me to welcome emotions as friends? Are you for real?

Alex held the silence.

Wait, maybe things would be easier if I accepted doubt as my friend, allowed it to tell me its story, then moved on.

'I understand what you are saying, Alex. I thought it was weird at first, but I guess it makes sense. I do have a question, though. If doubt is my friend, why does it make me feel so bad?'

'Is doubt making you feel bad, or is that how you are responding to doubt?'

Woah! Where did that come from?

'What do you mean?'

'Well, no one teaches us to be aware of our emotions or how to listen to them. So, we ignore them. And when they go unnoticed, we can't navigate them. Our emotions take control. Perhaps doubt is taking control. Or perhaps you haven't noticed other emotions present. When we pay attention to our emotions and understand why they are occurring, we can make choices about how we use them. Then they don't run ahead without us.'

'That makes sense, I guess.'

More silence.

'Where are you at now when it comes to doubt, Maggie?'

'Doubt is sending me a message when I am unsure of how to proceed because things are new to me. When doubt speaks to me, I interpret that as not trusting myself. Perhaps the lack of trust is because I am unsure. I don't trust myself to know the answers. But I do trust myself to work out a plan. Sometimes, working it out will involve asking people for help, and that's okay. When doubt leads me to hesitate, I can plan how to work things out.'

'That sounds great. So, what would help you now in our conversation?'

'I am comfortable with everything I have learnt, and it makes sense. I just don't know if I can act on it. The ideas are in my head but not my body, if that makes sense.'

'Are you open to exploring doubt and the body a little further, Maggie?'

'Yes, that sounds useful.'

'Great. Well, I invite you to stand up and find a spot.'

Maggie chose a spot closer to the window and closed her eyes.

'Imagine a time when you experienced doubt. What do you notice in your doubt body?'

'There is some tension, especially across my forehead.'

'What about your breathing and posture?'

'My breathing is shallow, also fast. I am not standing quite to full height, and my torso isn't straight. It's kind of concave.'

'Good. Now, let's stop and shake the emotions off. Jiggle your body and shake your hands, then take a step to the side and give yourself time to process what you experienced. We can explore this some more when you are ready.'

When Maggie was ready, she said, 'Wow, that was quite interesting. I hesitated and questioned what I was going to do.'

'Sounds helpful. So, where are you at?'

'That was a useful exercise because it allowed me to see doubt in slow motion. This enabled me to become aware of doubt, watch it, understand it and work with it.'

'Fabulous! How will your body be when you are at peace with doubt, when you trust yourself to work things out? What is happening in your body?'

Maggie spoke slowly, pausing between observations.

'My body is more upright. I am taller. My chest is open. My breathing is slowing. I am competent. I trust myself to work it out.'

Alex smiled and said, 'Outstanding! I invite you to stop and shake that off now. What helped you make peace with doubt?'

'It helped to slow my breathing. Also, elongating my spine and lifting my head made it easier to be at peace with doubt.'

'Would that be enough?'

'Yes.'

'I want to check in with you. Where are you at with this now?'

'I am quite comfortable with doubt. I am ready to stop.'

'Excellent! What declaration will you make?'

'Doubt is my friend, and I trust myself to work things out.'

'Fantastic! Well done, Maggie!'

The Learning

Doubt can be debilitating. We start by being unsure of how to proceed when something is new to us. We hesitate and question what we are doing. Before long, we become caught in a cycle, stuck and unable to act. From the outside, the solution may seem simple: either believe in yourself or stop doubting yourself and move on. However, life isn't always so simple.

What is doubt?

In *The Field Guide to Emotions: A Practical Orientation to 150 Essential Emotions*, Dan Newby and Curtis Watkins (2019) label doubt as an emotion. They propose it tells us we are unsure of how to proceed because the situation is new to us, suggesting the purpose of doubt is to help us focus on preparation. This makes sense. If something is new to us and we are unsure of how to proceed, our doubt-induced hesitation enables us to approach with caution, giving us time to prepare for the unknown.

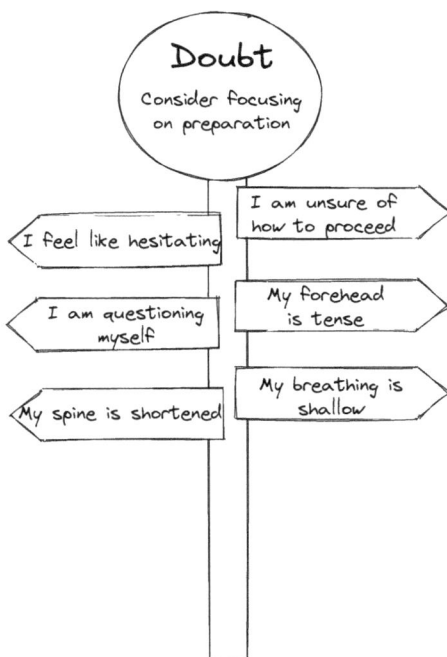

Figure 9: *Doubt is a sign we are unsure of how to proceed*

Doubt doesn't mean we can't do something; it just means we are unsure if or how we will do it. Therefore, doubt is a sign that shows us we are uncertain and need to prepare.

The key to understanding doubt is using the signs of doubt to guide us rather than allowing doubt to become a way of life. Figure 9 shows an example of the signs doubt may provide us. We can notice doubt from the stories we are telling ourselves, the actions it inclines us to take, and how our body is responding. When we notice these signs, we can choose how we use them. We may view the signs as a reason to ask for help or an opportunity to break the task into achievable chunks. We may use the signs to prepare for the task or to shift our Way of Being so it serves us in completing the task. By listening to doubt's message, we develop an awareness of what doubt means for us. Awareness brings choice, and choice brings the ability to interact more freely with ourselves and others.

Time-out to practise

1. Where are you noticing doubt in your life?
2. What is doubt telling you?
3. How will you use doubt's message to inform your next steps?

How to shift our stories of doubt

At the beginning of her conversation, Maggie believed doubt was limiting her and was, therefore, wrong. A turning point occurred when Maggie discovered doubt was appearing for a reason. Doubt had a message. Maggie listened to the message to understand what doubt was telling her. Changing our over-arching story of why doubt is present can be a critical step. This involves accepting doubt, treating it as a friendly sign rather than something to be feared, and understanding the message it brings.

When we operate from any emotion, we tell ourselves stories generated by the emotion. One story from doubt is, 'I don't know how to proceed because this is new to me'. Other stories might also be present, depending on our Way of Being. By becoming curious about what stories are present, we can understand how they are serving us and how we can shift to more useful stories. For example, one of Maggie's stories was she didn't trust herself to know the answers. After some reflection, Maggie could change her story from 'I don't trust myself to know the answers' to 'I trust myself to work out the next step'. This was enough for Maggie to progress.

Different stories become possible when we are curious about the stories we hold and why we are holding them. So, the question becomes, 'For the sake of what am I holding this story?' When we can answer that question, we develop the awareness needed to move forward. From there, we create possibility.

At times, a slight change in our story will be enough. Sometimes, finding a new story also means exploring our moods and emotions, and body. This will depend on how we interpret the situation.

Time-out to practise

1. What stories are you telling yourself *about* doubt?
2. What stories are you telling yourself *from* doubt?
3. For the sake of what are you holding these stories?
4. What alternative stories might help you?

What is trust?

While reflecting on doubt, Maggie found a connection to not trusting herself. In *Building trust in business, politics, relationships, and life*, Solomon and Flores (2001) suggest trust is a process relating to how we manage our commitments.

Our ability to trust comes from our Way of Being. From our Way of Being, we form opinions about ourselves and others, and these opinions inform how ready we are to trust.

Maggie assessed herself as not competent in her job. Competence is one of four judgements that Flores (2012) proposes drives our willingness to trust:

- sincerity
- reliability
- competence
- engagement.

We may not be aware we are applying the four judgements of trust. That's because they sit in the background, helping us assess the level of risk associated with trusting in each situation. Notably, we need only meet the judgements of trust deemed important to the task and not necessarily all judgements.

Maggie believed her level of competence was inadequate for the required task. Since competence was important to Maggie, she did not trust herself to complete the task. In the case of competence, it helps to ask why this judgement is important for the task at hand and whether the standard of competence we are applying is useful. Self-trust is not a measure of who we are. Self-trust depends on the standards we apply to a situation.

When we choose not to trust someone, we are not making a character judgement. Rather, trust is our opinion of whether we can rely on someone in a specific circumstance. A lack of trust in someone doesn't mean the person is bad. It means we have decided not to trust them based on the opinions we have formed about a specific situation. The same is true when we choose not to trust ourselves.

By understanding why we aren't trusting ourselves, we create the possibility of changing our level of self-trust. Table 5 offers questions we can ask to help understand how we are using the four judgements to inform our decision to trust ourselves. When we draw attention to these questions, we introduce choice into how we trust ourselves. The crucial question with trust is whether we can trust the person (or ourselves) to complete the task. We are interested in assessing the judgements of trust relevant to the task. We are not interested in forming opinions about moral qualities.

Judgement	Questions I might ask myself
• Sincerity	• Am I genuine in my commitment to this task? • Will my words to myself align with my words to others?
• Reliability	• Will I complete the task on time and to the required standard?
• Competence	• Do I have the skills, knowledge and experience required to complete the task?
• Engagement	• Do I understand and commit to what matters to me?

Table 5: *Applying the four judgements of trust to ourselves*

Newby and Watkins (2019) suggest the story we tell ourselves from trust relates to the level of risk we are prepared to take. When we offer trust, we accept the perceived level of risk involved in the interaction. Our perception of risk will change depending on the situation. We may trust someone to house-sit for us, yet not trust them to mind our children depending on how we assess risk according to the four trust judgements in each situation. Once we understand how we are responding to each question in Table 5, we can understand how to reduce risk and increase our level of self-trust.

How can we use trust to help counter doubt? Newby and Watkins (2019) suggest trust is a risk assessment and doubt is being unsure of how to proceed. Their suggestion indicates a link: doubt makes us unsure of how to proceed, potentially increasing the risk we associate with taking action. If we assess the risk as high, we may create further uncertainty about how to proceed, which could prevent us from moving forward.

Maggie asked herself, 'What do I trust myself to do in this situation?' She spoke of trusting herself to work things out, shifting her story from one centred on doubt to one centred on what she could achieve. We may also consider trusting ourselves to:

- ask for help
- collaborate with others
- admit we don't know
- create a plan
- delegate a task.

When focusing on where we can trust ourselves, we are focusing on the risk we will accept to accomplish the task at hand.

Time-out to practise

Identify a situation in which you don't trust yourself.

- Which of the four judgements of trust is informing your opinion of not trusting yourself?
- What do you trust yourself to do to help move the situation forward?

What other emotions can help us move forward from doubt?

Emotions move us to action. If we cannot take a specific action, another emotion may be useful. For example, doubt inclines us towards hesitating. If we are operating from doubt, we may find it difficult to engage with others. Other emotions, such as trust, guide us towards interacting with ourselves and others, and may be a useful addition to our Way of Being. Let's consider some other emotions that can be helpful in moving beyond doubt.

Faith

Newby and Watkins (2019) claim faith allows us to believe something without having evidence. It is important to note that

Newby and Watkins (2019) do not link faith to a god or religion but simply to not needing evidence. In everyday life, examples of faith could be:

- A job seeker believing they are suitable for a job that has been advertised, even though they have no evidence of how they would fit into the new organisation or how their skills may align with the new role.
- An Australian who believes they can drive in America with no evidence of their ability to drive on the opposite side of the road.
- A person believing they will have a great time at the opera with no evidence of having ever enjoyed the opera.
- A person believing they can achieve something new without evidence of whether this is true.

Let me share with you a personal experience of faith as an emotion in an everyday situation. A few years ago, I made seafood paella for friends for lunch. I had never made paella before. In fact, I had only tasted paella once. There was no evidence my attempt at cooking paella would be successful. Yet, I committed to a belief that I could make it. So, guided by faith in my ability to cook a dish for the first time, I invited my friends over and gave it a go. My belief did not involve a god or religion. I simply had faith in my ability to cook paella for my friends without evidence this was true.

Faith may have helped me cook a seafood paella for friends, but how can faith help us when we are operating from doubt? The key lies in what we will believe without evidence. Helpful questions to ask ourselves are:

- What am I willing to believe without evidence?
- What would enable me to commit to this belief?

Time-out to practise

Think of a situation where believing without evidence would be useful.

1. What shifts to your stories would allow you to believe without evidence?
2. How would believing without evidence occur in your body?
3. How could you shift your Way of Being to one that allowed you to believe without evidence?

Prudence

A few years ago, I visited a customer whose office was in a bush setting. A sign on the pathway leading to the front door read, 'Beware of snakes at the front of the building'. The sign alerted me to the potential danger of snakes sunning themselves on the warm concrete pathway and made me proceed with caution. Newby and Watkins (2019) claim when we are aware of a potential danger and choose to proceed with caution, we are operating from prudence.

Doubt inclines us towards uncertainty in terms of how to proceed. Being unsure can bring with it a perception of danger. Examples include:

*   loss of reputation
*   failure
*   loss of credibility
*   job loss
*   damage to relationships.

The purpose of doubt is to focus our attention on something new or unknown. We can use doubt to make us aware of the need to proceed cautiously and prudence to implement a step-by-step plan with regular check-ins at each stage. This helps us to prepare for new situations and proceed with care.

Time-out to practise

Think of a situation in which prudence was helpful.

1. How did prudence occur in your body?
2. How did prudence help you move forward?
3. What would help you add prudence to your current Way of Being?

Courage

Courage helps us act even though we may be fearful. Courage doesn't remove our fear; it allows us to act when fear is present. While doubt isn't fear, one can sometimes accompany the other. Some useful questions to ask ourselves when fear is present to encourage us to move forward with courage are:

- What do I fear?
- What am I telling myself about the fear?
- What can I tell myself that would help me embrace courage?
- What body would support me in taking action in the presence of fear?

Time-out to practise

Think of a situation in which you are doubting yourself.

1. How might faith be useful to you?
2. Where could prudence be a useful addition?
3. How might courage help you move forward?
4. How does courage occur in your body?

What emotions do we confuse with doubt?

We give labels to our emotions so we can make sense of our feelings and interpretations. However, sometimes our emotions can be quite similar. This can cause confusion when trying to determine which emotion is present, making it difficult to choose the most useful action to take.

Common candidates for confusion with doubt are fear, anxiety and uncertainty because they can feel somewhat similar. However, each emotion will incline us to tell ourselves a different story and cause alternative inclinations for action. When labelling our emotions, we seek to understand our stories and inclinations for action, which we can do by asking ourselves what we are telling ourselves and what actions our emotions incline us towards. Once we understand which emotions are present, we can ask ourselves *why* the emotion is present and *how* it is trying to help us.

Let us now explore fear, anxiety and uncertainty in more detail.

Fear

Our stories can help us identify whether fear or doubt is more likely to be present. That's because the stories we tell ourselves from each emotion are quite different:

- From fear, we tell ourselves something may harm us, and we know what that something is.
- From doubt, we tell ourselves we don't know how to proceed because something is new to us.

The inclination for action, however, is similar for both emotions, making it more difficult to differentiate between them.

- Fear inclines us towards avoiding a perceived danger.
- Doubt inclines us to hesitate and second-guess ourselves.

If fear is present, we are focused on harm from an identified source. One common fear linked with doubt is fear of failure, although fear of failure is not the only possibility.

When looking at the actions our emotions incline us to take, the key to differentiating between doubt and fear is to understand whether we are hesitating or avoiding. If we are hesitating, we are most likely operating from doubt. If we are avoiding, then fear may be present.

Sometimes, both emotions may be present. If we can understand what each emotion is telling us, we can understand how to navigate the emotions and shift them if necessary.

Anxiety

In this book, I am using the word 'anxiety' to refer to an in-the-moment response to a situation that may occur in everyday life and not as a reference to a diagnosed anxiety disorder. Please keep this context in mind as you read on.

The stories we tell ourselves from both fear and anxiety involve the possibility of being harmed by a perceived danger. However, the type of danger is different for each emotion. With fear, we know what we believe might harm us. With anxiety, however, we believe something may harm us, but we have not identified what that could be. Fear is being on a hike and believing a snake could bite us. Anxiety is being on a hike and believing *something* may harm us.

Just as anxiety is often confused with fear, it is also commonly confused with doubt. Anxiety tells us we believe an unknown source may harm us, whereas doubt tells us we are unsure of how to proceed because something is new to us. We can determine whether doubt or anxiety is present by asking ourselves whether the story is one of being harmed (anxiety) or of being unsure (doubt).

The way doubt and anxiety incline us to action is similar. However, there are subtle differences:

- Anxiety inclines us to worry and self-protect.
- Doubt inclines us to hesitate and second-guess ourselves.

The key is to ask ourselves whether we feel like worrying and self-protecting or hesitating and second-guessing ourselves.

Uncertainty

The stories we tell ourselves from uncertainty and doubt are also similar:

- From uncertainty, we tell ourselves we cannot easily predict or decide.
- From doubt, we tell ourselves we are unsure about how to proceed.

To understand our stories, we need to know whether we are unsure about how to proceed with something new or unable to decide. The more familiar we are with a situation, the more certain we are about how to proceed. However, if the story we are telling ourselves is coming from a place of uncertainty, being familiar with a situation may not change our ability to decide. We are inclined to hesitate from both doubt and uncertainty. This means we must understand why we are hesitating, which links back to the stories we are telling ourselves.

Time-out to practise

Identify a situation in which you appeared to be doubting yourself.

1. What stories were present?
2. What actions were you inclined towards taking?
3. Where in your body did you notice the presence of fear, anxiety or uncertainty?

Doubt and the body

Our body gives us many clues about how we are interpreting the world in any given moment. When we notice these clues, we create the possibility of identifying emotions we may not have realised were present or shifting our body and, therefore, our Way of Being.

Doubt, like all emotions, will provide some clues via our body. The first step in understanding those clues is to notice them. By becoming curious about how our body is holding doubt and what actions doubt is making available to us, we can gain insights into how we are being in the world and how we would like to be. For example, doubt inclines us towards second-guessing ourselves. So, we could ask ourselves what is happening in our body that enables us to second-guess ourselves. For example, where are we tense? How is our breathing? What sensations are present? Is our body open or withdrawn? Is our spine elongated or short?

All the above factors influence the actions our body can take. If we find that we are second-guessing ourselves but want to take a different action, we may need to shift our body in order to achieve that. We do that by understanding what elements of our current body configuration are helping us and what would be useful to change. Maggie and Alex explored this in their conversation, with Maggie discovering it was helpful to lengthen her spine, deepen her breathing and open her chest. When she explored how her body could change, she did so in consideration of the story she wanted to change. She sought to understand what body would support her in a story of 'I trust myself to work out the next step'.

Time-out to practise

Identify a situation in which you doubt yourself.

1. How does doubt appear in your body?
2. What actions would you like to take that your doubt body doesn't allow?
3. How could you adjust your body to enable you to take your desired actions?

A Deeper Reflection

Think of a situation in which you are currently doubting yourself. Write out or type up the stories you are telling yourself about the situation. Don't edit or censor your writing. Instead, note down everything that comes to mind in a stream-of-consciousness approach. Read through your written notes to answer the following questions.

1. What stories are present? How do your stories link to the emotions that are present?
2. Circle any actions you feel like taking. How do these actions relate to the emotions you are operating from? What do your actions tell you about your Way of Being?
3. How is your body influencing your Way of Being?
4. What would help you move on from doubt?
5. What new stories would help you?
6. What are you willing to trust yourself to do?
7. What additional emotions would be helpful?
8. Practise your new Way of Being for this situation.
9. What declaration will you make from this new Way of Being?
10. What was happening for you as a learner while you were progressing through this chapter?

Key Points

- Doubt shows us where it might be useful for us to prepare for something new.
- Trust is an assessment of the risk we are prepared to accept.
- We use the four judgements of trust – sincerity, reliability, competence and engagement – to determine whether we trust ourselves and others.
- Emotions signal how we are interpreting the world.
- When we understand emotions, we can choose how we use them.
- Some emotions are easily confused with doubt, and it is helpful to know the difference.

CHAPTER 7

How can emotions help me in my everyday life?

The Story

I feel awful. I mean, some things are better at work, but I can't help wondering why I am bothering. This whole learning and growing thing is never-ending. And I am always changing myself to accommodate others. Everyone else is oblivious to their actions and seems to get away with misbehaving. So, what's the point?

Why am I always the one to change?

Why can't others take responsibility for their actions?

Why are my shoulders so tense? Not to mention the butterflies in my stomach.

Everything is tense and overwhelming.

Walking up the path to Alex's door, Maggie took a deep breath.

Well, here goes. I hope I can hold myself together.

As she knocked on the door, Maggie envied Alex for having a business that enabled him to work from home.

'Hey, Maggie! Come in!'

'Hi, Alex. How are you?'

'Great, thanks! Today is such a beautiful day.'

Alex, you are always so positive. How on earth do you do it?

'So, what would you like to talk about today?'

Everything. It's all too much. I hope I don't cry.

Maggie's gaze was fixed on the garden for what felt like an eternity as she mustered the courage to speak.

'After our last conversation, I explored doubt and trust and applied what we discussed. That went well, but I am not great today. Work is toxic. I am experiencing a thousand different emotions, and I can't name any of them. I don't enjoy being this way. I am stuck in a cycle of yuckiness, for want of a better word, and I am not enjoying work at all.'

Well, I said it. Now Alex will think I am crazy.

Maggie focused on the birdbath in the garden, still hoping she wouldn't cry.

Alex didn't speak straight away.

Eventually, he smiled and said, 'The weather is glorious! There is a fabulous little lake down the road. Would you like to walk and talk?'

What a relief! A walking conversation means no eye contact.

'Sounds great.'

As they walked, Maggie composed herself. Alex was silent.

'It must be wonderful to live near a lake.'

'Yes, I try to come here a few times a week.'

Maggie appreciated the more casual conversation. It helped her relax.

Alex spoke again. 'What would you like to talk about?'

Maggie inhaled.

'Last time, we talked about doubt. I learnt so much and enjoyed putting everything into action. I mean, I am still not perfect at managing doubt, but doubt is no longer owning me. That is a vast improvement.'

'Sounds like you have made progress there, which is great. What else has been happening to make you feel the way you do today?'

Where do I begin?

Walking helped Maggie collect her thoughts. Once she started speaking, everything seemed to tumble out of her mouth.

'I watched myself and others at work, and I realised we lack leadership. Yes, my tasks are unfamiliar, and I am unsure how to move forward. There is a lot I can learn. But the behaviour of our leaders is abhorrent and contributes to my fear, uncertainty and doubt. They provide no direction. They rant when they don't get what they want. They don't commit, and they don't take ownership. Yet, they expect the rest of us to work things out without offering support. I am making myself sick with anxiety about a situation caused by sub-standard leadership!'

Maggie took a breath to recompose herself. Alex remained silent, giving her the space to continue.

'I am trying to change myself, but why am I doing this to make the world easier for everyone else? What's in this for me? These people need to understand their impact on others, do their jobs and own their behaviours. They shouldn't be exempt from changing their ways of being, either. I am not the only person responsible. They assume they are in the right, but their behaviour is wrong. I resent suffering and putting myself through hell trying to figure out how to function in a workplace where our leaders can't lead!'

Maggie's voice quivered.

'You appear to be holding a few opinions, Maggie,' said Alex.

'Yes, I guess so.'

'How are these opinions helping you?'

As they walked beside the lake, a pelican distracted Maggie from her thoughts.

Oh gosh, a pelican! They are the most beautiful birds and such a joy to watch.

'Perhaps it is wrong to have opinions, Alex, but I can't help taking pleasure in discovering not everything is my fault. These managers also play a role in the debacle that is my work.'

'Opinions aren't right or wrong, Maggie. They just are. It is fine to hold an opinion so as long as those opinions are serving you. You said your opinions are helping you to see that the situation is not all your fault. Can you explain what you mean by that?'

'I am struggling in this job, and I am in a cycle of blaming myself. Some of my challenges are my doing. However, since paying attention to my Way of Being and the world around me, I can see I am struggling in an environment made challenging by others. My opinions help me understand there are more people at fault than just me. Others are contributing to my situation as well.'

'Why does that matter?'

Maggie smiled at a passerby being led along the path by their golden retriever.

'It means I am not always wrong. And if I am not always wrong, I must sometimes be right. My Way of Being is contributing to some of my struggles, but I am also reacting to the behaviours of others. I can't help but be relieved by that.'

'Why relief?'

'It means I can trust myself a little more because I am not the only cause of my current struggles. But I am still unsure of how to handle these behaviours. To me, the behaviours are unacceptable, so this isn't only about me and my own challenges. It's also about how others are behaving.'

'Wow. Sounds powerful.'

> Woah, when did I become insightful? But I still don't understand why these people can get away with behaving this way.

'What emotions are present besides relief?' Alex asked.

'I am trying to change who I am being at work because I think this will be useful for me when I interact with others. However, I am changing my Way of Being to accommodate people whose ways of being allow them to be jerks. And I resent that they don't seem to realise they are being jerks. Why can't they change their ways of being? Why should I be the only one to change?'

'Well, we can only control our own actions and behaviours. We can't control or change others. However, when our Way of Being shifts, others sometimes respond by shifting their Way of Being and behaviours too.

'When we are interacting with others, we are each forming our own interpretations and stories. We all experience conversations that don't go so well, and we are all pretty good at blaming others or assuming they are wrong. When we do this, we can't always bring about change. When we accept our role in our interactions and explore the shifts we can make within ourselves, we can shift our Way of Being to create new outcomes. Sometimes, those around us will shift their behaviours in response to our behaviours changing. They may not even realise they are doing so.

'It sounds as though your leaders use a leadership approach that isn't always helpful. You can't control how they are being. You can only control how you are. Does that make sense?'

'Yes, it does, but I still resent it,' said Maggie.

'And what do you think resentment might be telling you?'

Maggie inhaled, staring towards the horizon as she gathered her thoughts.

'I think resentment is telling me that the situation is unfair.'

'How will you use this message? What would help you?'

It would help if these managers did the right thing.

Maggie took a deep breath and continued. 'Okay, the way these managers are behaving is not right. They get away with this behaviour. They are not aware of their impact on others. It is unfair.'

'How is this story of resentment helping you?'

Sometimes, Alex, your questions are so hard.

'Well, I guess I can now identify what I consider as unfair.'

'And…?'

I don't know. I am making this up as I go.

'This helps me find a boundary. I mean, when I interpret something as unfair, I am creating a boundary between fair and unfair.'

'That's interesting. What will you do with this boundary?'

Maggie stared at the lake for what seemed like a long time.

Alex is incredible at remaining silent.

'Resentment is showing me a boundary, which is also helping me see how the behaviours I allow from others contribute to the situation. The blame is not mine alone. I can take some pressure off myself, but I also need to set boundaries around the behaviours that I allow.'

I am unsure of where that came from, but I like this growing awareness. Wow!

Maggie spoke again, 'Oh, my goodness, I am not sure where I pulled that from, but it makes sense!'

Alex smiled before saying, 'Yes, it sounds like a helpful realisation.'

'It *is* helpful. I have been in a cycle of resentment. Nothing changes when I am in that cycle. In fact, I suffer more. If I listen to resentment, it will help me set a boundary for what I will accept. And that would help me create different outcomes.'

'What would help you set the boundary?'

No idea.

Maggie remained silent. Alex waited.

'Would you mind giving me a clue?' Maggie asked. 'I am unsure of how to answer you.'

'I wonder what you can look for as a sign of resentment being present. What is happening in your body when you are experiencing resentment?'

Maggie and Alex both paused, stepping off the path so Maggie could reflect on resentment.

Maggie closed her eyes, imagining resentment in her body.

'The most obvious sensation is stiffness in my shoulders and jaw.'

'How might you shift the stiffness?'

Maggie closed her eyes again.

'A deep breath loosens my jaw, and now it seems easier to loosen my shoulders.'

'And what difference are these shifts making?'

'The resentment has shifted a little.'

'Would it be possible for you to set a boundary?'

'How?'

'Depends on what boundary. Sometimes, saying something might be useful. Other times, doing or not doing something will help draw a line. Or, perhaps not responding at all might be a useful approach.'

'A lot of managers at work are almost combative in their approach. How am I meant to react to combative behaviour? At the moment, I accept their behaviour and say nothing because there is no other way. They keep being aggressive because I am allowing them to do so. How do I set a boundary for their behaviour when I can't control what they do?'

'Well, let's explore your Way of Being. You say there is no other way. When you assess these people as being combative, is your body diminished, or at full height, or something else?'

'Diminished.'

Diminished, beaten, broken. They're all the same, aren't they?

'What would help you to enlarge your body, remain strong and send a different message?'

'A deep breath might be a good starting point, but I am unsure what else I can do.'

'Can I offer something?'

'Sure.'

'Well, I wonder whether the emotion of dignity would help you. When we are working from dignity, our story is "I choose". Do you find this story useful?'

Wow!

'Dignity didn't occur to me as an emotion, but yes, it might be useful,' said Maggie.

'Would you like to try dignity now?'

'Yes, I would.'

Maggie stood up, choosing a spot a little closer to the lake. Alex followed.

As Maggie closed her eyes, Alex said, 'Imagine you are experiencing the behaviour of your managers. As you are doing so, I invite you to say to yourself, "I choose". You can add more words if you like but allow the story to be "I choose". As you do so, pay attention to your body, specifically what shift in your body will allow you to believe you are choosing.'

Good Lord, here I am, practising different body postures on the side of a lake, out in public! Things I never expected to be doing.

After a couple of minutes, Maggie spoke.

'My body is expanded – relaxed but ready to speak up. I am taller and wider, more open, perhaps. The stiffness and tension are no longer present.'

'If one of your combative managers approached you right now, what would you do?'

'I wouldn't let their behaviour worry me as much. I would stand tall and hold my ground.'

'How would that be helpful?'

'The behaviour of my managers leaves me feeling as though I don't matter. Now, I matter. I have decided, and I matter.'

'And how would you shift your Way of Being at work so you matter?'

Maggie stared at nothing in particular as she gathered her thoughts.

'I would allow the stiffness in my body to be my sign.'

'Great. So, we talked about relief, resentment and dignity. Where are you at right now? What would you like to discuss next?'

Alex and Maggie started walking again.

'I am also experiencing anger, which I know is wrong,' said Maggie.

'Why is anger wrong?'

'I become nasty when I allow myself to be angry. Besides, everyone knows anger is wrong. No one appreciates anger.'

'If emotions contain a story, what might anger's story be?' asked Alex.

'When I listen to the anger, all I can hear is that the managers are wrong.'

'Well, one interpretation of anger is that it tells us when we see something as morally wrong.'

'Ah, okay. But I still don't enjoy anger.'

'Can I offer something, Maggie?'

'Sure.'

'We learn to label emotions as "right" or "wrong", and we judge ourselves for experiencing the "wrong" emotions. A more useful interpretation of emotions is that they are signs of how we are interpreting the world. When you understood your stories from a place of relief, resentment and dignity, working with them became possible. We can say the same with anger. It is not wrong to interpret the world in a way that leads to anger. Sometimes, anger is useful and necessary. Anger shows us what we interpret as morally wrong and, by association, what we interpret as morally right. If we don't experience anger, how do we identify what is morally right or wrong for us?'

'That's fair, but I am not nice when I am angry.'

'How we respond to anger comes down to our choices for using anger. We aren't taught how to listen to what our emotions are telling us, so we aren't aware of what to do with them. Emotions predispose us to take particular actions. If we don't understand the signs of an emotion, we will miss what the emotion is telling us. Instead, we tend to go in the direction the emotion points us towards. Anger predisposes us to punish the source of the wrongdoing, so we behave in a way that supports punishing others. If we understand our emotions, we open ourselves to greater choice in how we respond. We don't allow the emotion to lead us.'

Woah. My head just exploded. So, anger isn't wrong? When did that happen?

'Wow. That's huge. So, are you saying I could listen to anger and understand what I am interpreting as morally wrong?' asked Maggie.

'I am suggesting it might be a useful approach if you would like to try it.'

'Next time I experience anger at work, I will try to pause and listen to it.'

'Sounds like a plan. When you listen to it, you might find out why it is present. You may even work out what actions to take, which could include shifting to another emotion if that is useful.'

'Gosh, I have a lot to learn about emotions.'

'To be honest, most of us do. Now, we are almost back at my house. Where are you at in the conversation right now?'

Blown away by your take on emotions, to be honest.

'This conversation has helped me understand what is happening at work. It has made me realise that I am judging my managers. While they deserve some of my judgements, I can also see how I can change my behaviours. Understanding dignity has helped because it means I can tackle some challenges without compromising myself. I will stand my ground and speak up when needed. I won't compromise who I want to be. Before I arrived here today, my whole body felt like one enormous ball of emotions. But I now know I can learn to understand my emotions and use them to add value to my interactions with others.'

'You will become more familiar with your emotions as you interact with them more. Also, keeping an emotional diary can be helpful. Even if you can't name the emotion, you can note what is happening in your body, what story is present, what actions you want to take and what the emotion wants you to achieve.'

'Brilliant, thank you!'

Did I just agree to keep an emotional diary? Not something I would expect from me.

'What declaration would you like to make before we finish?'

'I am a curious and focused explorer of my emotions.'

'Perfect.'

'Thanks for the walk. Pure genius. My entire Way of Being shifted.'

'You are welcome. Sometimes, shifting our Way of Being can be as simple as shifting our focus and energy to something new.'

The Learning

As humans go through life, we learn about emotions from our culture, upbringing and others in society. For example, as a child, I learnt pride was wrong. Maggie conveyed similar learning when she described anger as wrong. In both cases, our experience of life provided us with rules for using our emotions.

The rules we create for using our emotions inform the actions we take. In my earlier years, I learnt pride was conceited, arrogant and boastful. Consequently, I created a rule that prevented me from experiencing pride. Yet, Newby and Núñez (2017) claim the story we tell ourselves from pride is, 'I want to tell others I have done something good'. Their interpretation suggests the rules I created for pride did not allow me to tell others about my achievements. How do we acknowledge our efforts if we cannot speak up when we believe we have done well?

Since acknowledging my achievements was 'wrong', I found other ways to be acknowledged. For example, I would belittle myself in front of others to receive their positive responses. This behaviour was not deliberate. I had learnt to operate this way on autopilot because pride was not an option for me. The rules created by my early learning of pride informed my behaviour well into adulthood. At that point, I realised pride being 'wrong' was one option, but not the only one.

We may assume our emotional rules to be 'the truth', as I did with pride. Yet these rules are opinions learnt as we progress through life. Opinions are not true or false, although we may fall into the trap of holding them as the truth. When considered true, opinions become myths. Emotional myths influence how we view, use and convey our emotions. They provide boundaries for how we partake in life and remove possibility. Common myths about emotions include:

- Emotions only occur when we are being emotional.
- Emotions have no purpose.
- Emotions are positive and negative, or good and bad.

- It is wrong to experience negative emotions.
- We must control or suppress negative emotions.

Most of us don't learn how to navigate our emotions. Instead, we follow the lead of each emotion, unaware we are doing so. As a result, we create outcomes that may not be ideal. As humans trying to make sense of the world, we blame our emotions for unhelpful consequences. If we don't like the outcome, we impose rules for interacting with our emotions to avoid similar outcomes in the future. In doing so, we create and live in a perpetual cycle of emotional myths.

We can create choice when we challenge our emotional myths and rules. Some questions to assist with that include:

- What makes an emotion positive or negative?
- Who decides which emotions are right and wrong?
- Why are some emotions considered wrong?
- Why are some emotions considered right?

Time-out to practise

Reflect on your past learning of emotions.

- What myths did you learn?
- How are your myths informing your emotional responses?
- How are your myths limiting you?
- How would it help to challenge your myths?

Debunking the emotional myths

Newby and Núñez (2017) use the etymology of the word 'emotion' to describe emotions as 'that energy that moves us to take action'. We are always taking action. Even when we are doing nothing, we are doing something. For us to do something, we need the 'energy that moves us' to be present. Since emotions are the energy that moves us, they must always be with us, even when we don't notice them. Newby and Núñez (2017) also counter the idea of emotions being without purpose, claiming we can break down the purpose of each emotion in three distinct ways:

- The story we tell ourselves while in the emotion.
- The action the emotion inclines us to take.
- The purpose of the emotion.

The three parts of each emotion offer information about how we are interpreting the world. For example, if we see a snake while hiking, we might experience fear, which tells us we perceive the snake as a danger. Our fear of the snake will incline us towards avoiding the snake. The purpose of fear is to help us avoid the perceived danger of the snake. How would we understand what may harm us if we didn't experience fear?

Several emotional myths describe emotions as good or bad, creating further myths to prevent us from experiencing the 'bad' emotions. Since each emotion tells us how we are seeing the world, how can it be bad to receive its message? We may not like how we feel or behave from the emotion, but that doesn't make the emotion bad.

Newby and Núñez (2017) claim each emotion inclines us toward a specific action. If we are unaware of the emotion's presence, the emotion can take control, leaving us with little say in what we do. We take the action our emotions incline us towards, achieving whatever outcome we achieve. And then we blame our actions on our emotions because we forget we have a choice in what we do. *Oh, you yelled at someone. Yes, anger makes us yell. Don't be angry and you won't yell.* This is like saying, 'I burnt myself cooking dinner, so I will no longer cook meals'! While this is a legitimate approach, eating salad every night may narrow your experience of the world. By refusing to cook, you would also be removing personal responsibility and placing it on the action of cooking hot meals. Is it appropriate to blame being burnt while cooking a hot meal on the hot meal? Wouldn't it make more sense to learn how to navigate cooking a hot meal?

How we interpret an emotion will set the rules we create for experiencing both the emotion and life. For example, anger tells us what we interpret as morally wrong or unjust. If we judge anger as bad, we limit ourselves by not allowing ourselves to be angry. How do we understand our standards for 'morally wrong' and 'unjust' if we don't experience anger?

Emotions exist in life as emotions. They only become good or bad when we label them 'good' or 'bad'. If we suppress them, we limit how we experience life and place the blame for our actions and behaviours on our emotions.

When we hold emotional myths as true, we open our emotions to judgement. These judgements guide our experience of life. By removing judgement and accepting our emotions as nothing more than emotions, we can learn to choose the actions we take. Doing so allows us to navigate our emotions in everyday life instead of being led by them.

Time-out to practise

Recall a time when you experienced a specific emotion during a conversation.

- What story were you telling yourself?
- How did the emotion occur in your body?
- What action did you want to take?
- What action did you take?
- Why did the emotion appear?
- What purpose was the emotion serving?

How can emotions help us?

Emotions are always with us, providing messages about how we are viewing the world. Each emotion informs the action we take. When we gain the ability to understand our emotions, we create flexibility and choice in how we respond to the everyday challenges of life.

In *Emotional Intelligence: Why it can matter more than IQ*, Daniel Goleman (1996) refers to emotions as the 'instant plans' we use in life, shaped by our learning, culture and experience. His reference reminds me of the time we forgot some friends were coming for a roast dinner. As a newly married couple with no children, we didn't have enough food in the house for an additional four people. We needed an instant plan. The plan turned out to be Chinese takeaway. It took a moment for everyone to adjust to not having a roast dinner. But then we pulled out the takeaway menu, ordered Chinese and had a thoroughly enjoyable evening.

Much like my instant plan helped us create a meal for our friends, emotions provide a plan for dealing with how we are interpreting the world at a particular point in time. Fear, for example, helps us create an instant plan for dealing with perceived danger. Gratitude helps us create an instant plan for seeing something as a gift. Doubt helps us create an instant plan for being unsure. Resignation helps us create an instant plan for when we assess there is no point in acting. Resentment helps create an instant plan for dealing with something we see as unfair. And so on.

How we invoke our instant plan will differ depending on our prior learning and our Way of Being. For example, Goleman (1996) claims that while losing a loved one will incline us towards sadness and grief, each of us will convey our sadness and grief differently based on our culture, learning and life experiences. Our actions will depend on how we interpret the sadness, the judgements we make, what we understand about the sadness and the messages we choose to take from it.

Emotions can run away from us and lead us when we ignore them. When we notice our emotions, we can listen to the messages they are telling us and understand why we are experiencing them. Doing so enables us to make deliberate choices about the actions we will take. The benefit gained from each emotion depends on how we choose to learn from the message it is giving us.

Time-out to practise

Recall a time when you were aware of experiencing a particular emotion.

- What instant plan did this emotion make available to you?
- How did the instant plan help you?
- If you experienced this situation in the future, how would you adjust the instant plan to serve you in a more useful way?

What is emotional literacy?

In *Emotional Literacy: Intelligence with a Heart,* Claude Steiner (2003) describes emotional literacy as being able to handle our emotions so they work *for* us rather than *against* us. Steiner (2003) offers improvement in personal power and quality of life for self and others as side-effects of emotional literacy. But what does this mean?

My grandfather did not read or write. He spoke English and understood grammar, yet he could not navigate the written word. This limited the actions he could take in life. He could not apply for a job where reading and writing were required. He could not read a menu and choose his own meal. He could not read to his children. My grandfather's literacy level prevented him from using written words to create what he wanted in life. Similarly, our emotional literacy can help or hinder us in our everyday lives.

Most of us are familiar with the more common emotions. Yet, our emotional literacy doesn't always allow our emotions to serve us. Often our prior learning gets in the way, or our emotions end up leading us because we don't know how to read them. When we lack emotional literacy, we get by but don't always create useful interactions. Outcomes are often random because they don't come from a place of awareness. Instead, they just happen. When we develop and grow our emotional literacy, we become more flexible in how we respond. We create the possibility of choice.

Imagine talking to someone who you feel talks down to you. You find their approach rude and condescending, and you don't enjoy the conversation. They seem to dismiss one of your ideas, and you have a sudden urge to yell at the person. What would you do?

Without emotional literacy, we respond based on our rules and prior learning. If we have a sudden urge to yell, we follow the lead and yell. If we don't want to yell, we might storm off, say something nasty, or suppress how we are feeling. Often these behaviours create other emotions as we try to navigate an outcome we didn't intend to create.

With emotional literacy, we can learn to ask questions. Instead of ignoring our emotions building up in our body and then reacting, we notice our emotions and ask ourselves questions. *What emotion am I feeling? Why is the emotion present? What is it telling me? Why is it telling me this? How might the other person be feeling? What are they trying to take care of for themselves? What am I trying to take care of for myself? What can I do other than yell or storm off? What is the best way to achieve a useful outcome?* As we explore these questions, we create clarity and choice. Whether we make a request, say nothing, walk off or yell, our action will be through deliberate choice.

Time-out to practise

Take a moment to focus on the emotions you are experiencing right now.

- Can you name the emotions?
- How are the emotions occurring in your body?
- What are your emotions telling you?
- Why are your emotions present?
- What actions are they inclining you towards?
- What actions will you choose to take from these emotions?

Creating choice from our emotions

As Antonio Damasio (1994) suggests in *Descartes' Error: Emotion, reason and the human brain*, how we interpret our emotions links to our Way of Being. Let's consider an example. If I am hiking and see a snake, my Way of Being might lead me to experience fear. On the other hand, if a herpetologist saw a snake while out walking, they might notice curiosity, wonder, excitement or even gratitude. Our different reactions to the same object suggest that it is not the snake creating our emotions. We are creating our emotions based on how we perceive the snake from our Way of Being, which supports the idea that our emotions come from *and* inform our Way of Being and the actions we take.

Sometimes, labelling our emotions is difficult. This is where paying attention to how each emotion occurs in our body is useful. Each emotion creates its own sensations and responses in our body. When we are aware of the sensations, we can become clearer on how to name the emotion.

Awareness creates choice, flexibility and new ways of taking action, including:

- making a request
- making a declaration
- holding a conversation
- changing or adding to our emotions
- making an offer
- removing ourselves from a situation
- doing nothing (if doing nothing is coming from a place of considered and deliberate choice).

Emotions signal how we are interpreting the world, much like street signs. As Figure 10 shows, if we fail to notice the street signs while driving, we will follow the road we are travelling and end up wherever it takes us. We may have wanted to go to the beach but arrived in the city because we removed choice when we became unaware of the signs. However, if we pay attention to the signs, we create the possibility of going to the beach, city or country. Noticing the sign gives us choice. In a similar way, if we don't notice the signs of an emotion, we take action without realising why because the emotion will lead us along the default path. When we pay attention to the signs, we create choice.

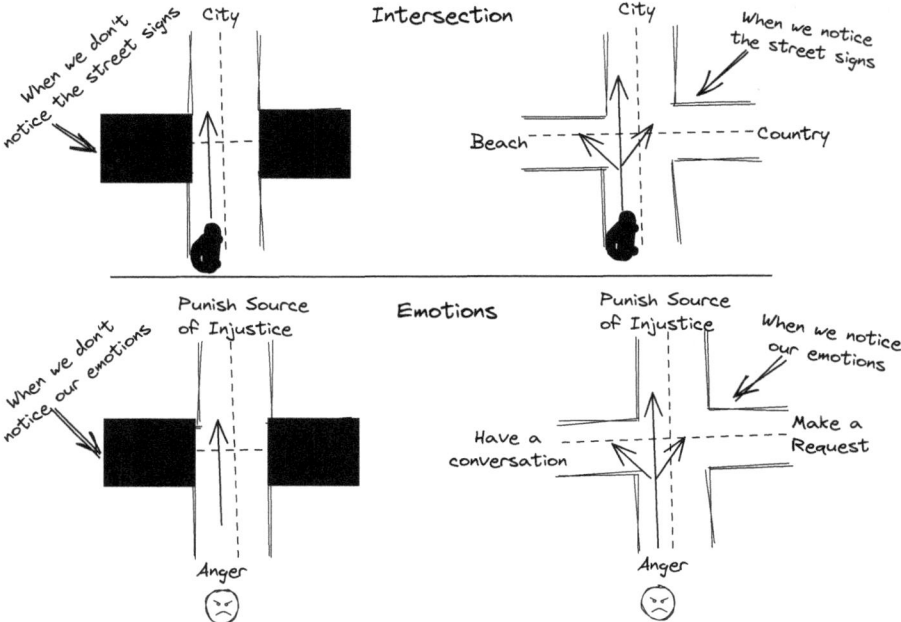

Figure 10: *Emotions are like street signs*

When driving, we don't remove the street signs pointing to destinations we don't like. We leave the sign intact. Even if we don't want to go to the city, the city sign provides information about the world we live in. Emotions are similar. It is legitimate to experience whatever emotion is present, even if we would prefer not to. Instead of ignoring it, we can listen to what the emotion is telling us and use the information to choose our next action.

Time-out to practise

Reflect on a situation that isn't going well for you.

- What emotional signs are present that you have not been noticing?
- How will you use the signs?
- How will paying attention to the signs shift the actions you choose to take?

Emotions and body

We label our emotions in language based on the sensations they create in our body. Because our emotions live in our body, we can use our body as a source of learning. With each emotion, there will be new sensations, shifts in our breathing, adjustments to our posture, areas of tension, changes in the shape of our spine, etc. If we pay attention to these subtle shifts, we can improve our emotional awareness and, therefore, our emotional literacy. It may even be possible to shift our emotions by shifting aspects of our body.

Time-out to practise

Take a moment to notice what is happening in your body.

- Is your spine elongated or shortened?
- What is the shape of your spine?
- Is your torso open or closed? Wide or concave?
- How are you holding your shoulders?
- What is the position of your neck and head?
- Do you notice any tension in your body? If so, where?
- How would you describe your breathing?
- What do you notice in your neck?
- Where are your feet?
- What sensations are present? How do they feel?
- What information is your body telling you about your emotions?
- What happens when you shift something in your body?

A Deeper Reflection

For the next week, you are invited to track your emotions in a journal.

1. Throughout each day, pay attention to your emotions and write what you notice in your journal.

2. At the end of each day, reflect on your learning and become curious about what your emotional experiences are offering you.

3. Once you feel comfortable exploring your emotions in your journal, try exploring your emotions during your interactions with others.

4. What was happening for you as a learner while you were progressing through this chapter?

Information you might include in your journal to support your learning includes:

- The name of the emotion.
- What you are saying to yourself.
- What you feel like doing.
- What is happening in your body.
- Why the emotion is present.
- What learning the experience offers you.

Key Points

- Emotions are always with us.
- We don't have to live from our emotional myths.
- Emotions comprise a story, an inclination for action and a purpose.
- Emotions are signs that show us how we are interpreting the world.
- When we understand our emotions, we create choice in our everyday interactions.
- Emotions live in our body, making the body a source of learning.

CHAPTER 8

Why am I finding this person difficult to deal with?

The Story

'So, how are things?' Alex asked at their next meeting.

'I found our last discussion about emotions useful.'

'How so?'

Maggie took her time to find the right words.

How do I explain?

'Pausing and trying to name my emotions was helpful. I don't always notice emotions when they are happening, but when I reflect on them after the event, I try to name them. Now, whenever I notice and name my emotions, I understand why I am experiencing them. For example, I struggle to interact resourcefully with one of my work colleagues. My whole body becomes tense whenever she comes near me, and I tell myself she is difficult. In fact, I'm ready for her to be difficult before she has even spoken. This week, I identified and named my reaction as resentment. When I asked myself why I feel this way, I realised it's because I don't like the way she speaks to people. I think she is aggressive and bullying and doesn't listen. I don't like those behaviours, so whenever I interact with her, I start from a place of resentment.'

'Interesting,' said Alex.

'Yes. But then I tried to think of the situation from her perspective. I am not sure she means to be aggressive and bullying. She doesn't realise how people interpret her actions. I realised my reaction to her says more about how *I* am interpreting her actions than it says about her. However, I struggle. I find her infuriating. But at least now, I take a deep breath and pause before reacting, which has been useful. I still don't like dealing with her, but I understand what is happening between us a little better now.'

'Well done, Maggie. It can take some effort to consider the perspective of others when we find their behaviour perturbing.'

'Thanks. I can't say I agree with her approach any more than before, but at least I can work with her.'

'You might never see eye to eye. However, understanding how you are both responding will influence your interactions. The goal of this work isn't to take the perfect action in every situation. The goal is to help you understand what is happening in your interactions so you can try to achieve the outcomes that best serve you and others.'

'I still need to remind myself that my focus should be on producing behaviours that serve me, not being perfect. But I'll get there.'

'Yes, you will. So, what would you like to talk about in our conversation today?'

Maggie gathered her thoughts in silence.

'This week, I would like to delve deeper into dealing with difficult people. I can't provide a specific example. I mean, sometimes I find the managers at work difficult because they would rather criticise than help. But this conversation isn't about work. I went to the supermarket earlier this week and saw a customer being difficult with a staff member. The staff member handled her well despite her abusive behaviour. I would not have handled it as well as the staff member, and I am curious to learn a useful way for me to respond in a similar situation in the future.'

I hope Alex doesn't think I'm silly to ask a question that isn't related to a specific issue. But I want to understand how I can deal with difficult people. If I had been dealing with the customer yesterday, my frustration would have shown. I am curious and want to understand how to deal with a difficult person in a more useful way in the future.

'What do you mean by "difficult people"?' asked Alex.

'Good question. To me, a difficult person is someone whose behaviour does not make it easy to get a useful outcome, someone whose behaviour I don't like or agree with.'

'What don't you like about a difficult person's behaviour?'

'Their behaviour is wrong.'

'Is it a fact that their behaviour is wrong, or is that your opinion?'

That's an interesting question.

Maggie inhaled as she thought of a response.

'It's my opinion.'

'If "wrong" is an opinion in this case, what would you say about "difficult"?'

Oh. I get it.

'Difficult is also an opinion.'

'Interesting.'

'Am I wrong to call the customer difficult?'

'No. You are offering an opinion, and opinions can't be right or wrong. Our opinions come from how we are interpreting the world. It is valid to form whatever opinion our Way of Being allows. However, it is important to be aware that the opinion exists because of how we are interpreting the world and not because of any properties within the person. You interpreted the customer as difficult because that is how your Way of Being led you to interpret her behaviour. Now that you realise "difficult" is your interpretation and not a truth about how a person is, you can make choices about how you use your opinion.'

'What do you mean when you say "difficult" isn't about how the person is?'

'You labelled the customer as difficult because you saw her as difficult. Another person might have labelled her as "right" or "friendly" or "nice". The different labels come from how you are each viewing the customer's actions, not from anything within her.'

'Good point. So, if "difficult" is an opinion, how do we use it?'

'We can choose what we do with our opinions, Maggie. Being able to view our opinions as opinions provides us with choice. Much of the traditional literature on dealing with difficult people place responsibility on the person we label as difficult. We declare our label as their problem because we assume they are the ones who are difficult, suggesting they must change. However, we are labelling them as difficult based on our interpretation of them. They may not even realise we assess them as difficult. Yet, we are expecting them to change. When we understand that we have assigned the label of "difficult" to the person, we create possibility. The two elements in the difficult person equation are the other person's behaviour and our interpretation of their behaviour. Our interpretation may change if they change their behaviour, but their behaviour may also shift. That all depends on how we use our interpretation.'

'Wow. I haven't thought of it that way before.'

Alex smiled.

'Describe your Way of Being during your supermarket visit yesterday. Why did the customer occur to you as difficult?'

Her behaviour was wrong. No one should yell at a staff member like she did.

Maggie paused for a moment as she reflected on the previous day.

'When the customer raised her voice, I labelled the customer as wrong. The way she made her complaint did not support a useful outcome. I wanted to defend the staff member.'

'What moods and emotions did you notice within you?'

'Anger, resentment and indignation. I wanted to rush forward and defend the staff member and stop the customer's poor behaviour.'

'What moods and emotions may have been present for the customer?'

Interesting question.

'Well, the customer appeared arrogant, disrespectful and unkind. However, to be fair, she had two small children with her, and the staff member kept her waiting for a while. Perhaps she felt frustrated. With the benefit of hindsight, I guess it's possible that she didn't intend to be disrespectful or difficult. Maybe she responded in the best way she knew how.'

'Sounds like useful learning. How would you relate this learning to work or other situations?'

'I would consider the other person's point of view and ask myself about their Way of Being. That might help me understand what led to their behaviour. If it served us to do so, I would also shift my Way of Being.'

'Wow, great insight. What if you didn't understand their Way of Being? What would you do then?'

I am unsure how to answer this question.

Alex waited.

'I guess if I didn't have any clues about their Way of Being, I could remain curious. I could also remind myself that "difficult" is an opinion and be mindful not to treat it as a truth. There might also be occasions when a conversation would be helpful.'

'Fantastic! So, I want to check; where are you at with this now?'

'I am ready to finish our conversation. I can view difficult people differently now, and I have learnt a new perspective that will be useful.'

'Before we finish up, let me ask you one more question. What emotions might be useful to include in your Way of Being to support you in working with someone you assessed as difficult?'

Maggie took a few moments to consider her response.

'Curiosity, compassion and courage. Curiosity has the potential to show me the other person's perspective. Compassion will help me understand the person, and courage will help me choose how to respond. I also wonder whether dignity might be helpful.'

'Fantastic! I can't wait to find out how this goes!'

The Learning

Facts and opinions

When we see someone as difficult, we assume the individual exists in the world as difficult in the same way a table exists in the world as a table. But is this really the case?

In Chapter 1, we talked about how humans can use language to describe what already exists in the world. For instance, as a society, we have a community-agreed standard for what defines a table. Anyone looking at an object can determine whether it is a table according to the agreed standard. This suggests the claim, 'this object is a table', will either be true or false. If the claim is true, the statement is a truth or fact. If the claim is false, we call it an untruth or falsehood. This applies to any statement we can evaluate as true or false using a community-agreed standard.

Not all interpretations are based on community-agreed standards, however. As we progress through life, we develop personal standards. Because each of us experiences life differently, our personal standards differ, suggesting our claims about the world will also differ. Referring to our example, what I claim is an ugly table, someone else may argue is stunning. No one is right or wrong. We are each declaring how we are viewing the table based on our personal standards. Whenever we apply personal standards, we are using opinions and not facts. Let's now look at opinions more closely.

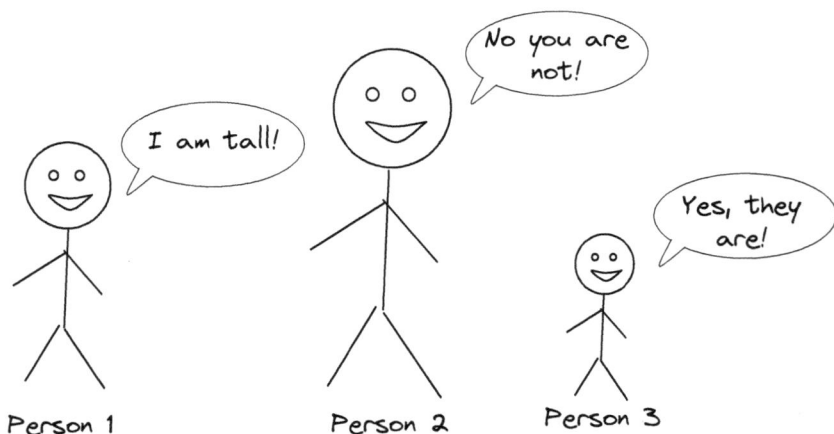

Figure 11: *Opinions cannot be true or false*

Figure 11 shows a conversation between Person 1, Person 2 and Person 3. Person 1 holds the opinion that they are tall. Person 2, a taller person, disagrees with Person 1. Person 3, who is shorter than Person 1, agrees with Person 1's opinion. No one in this conversation is right or wrong. Rather, each person is showing how they are seeing the world. So, how does this apply to a person we see as difficult?

When we label someone as difficult, we are doing so based on our personal standards, not a community-agreed standard. This means 'difficult' is an opinion, not a fact. If difficult is an opinion, we can say that people do not exist in *the* world as difficult. Rather, they exist in *our version* of the world as difficult.

It is not wrong for us to form an opinion of someone as difficult. We see life how we see it, and opinions help us create meaning from what we see. However, much can be learnt by asking ourselves why we are seeing someone as difficult. What in our Way of Being has us seeing the person as difficult? In this way, our opinions can be a source of learning.

WHAT IF LIFE CAME WITH A USER GUIDE?

Time-out to practise

Which of the following claims can we evaluate as facts or falsehoods, and which are opinions?

1. I am 165cm tall.
2. Their house is enormous.
3. The team leader was ten minutes late for our meeting today.
4. That person doesn't care about their job.

When we confuse opinions with fact

Facts place boundaries on what is possible. When we use facts or speak of 'what is', we are, by association, also speaking of 'what is not'. For example, it is a fact that Australia is a country. However, this also means Australia can't *not* be a country. For one claim to be a fact, another claim will be untrue. The same applies to all facts. For something to be true, something else must be false or not possible.

Conversely, opinions are a perspective and, therefore, can be neither true nor false. One opinion does not rule out another. Suppose we hold an opinion that someone is difficult. In that case, they can also be viewed as 'not difficult' by others or in different situations. For example, we may see a person as difficult when they order food in a restaurant yet see them as not difficult in other areas of life. Because opinions are a perspective, we can change them by shifting the standards, stories, moods and emotions, and body from which we are forming them.

Although opinions cannot be true or false, a trap we can fall into is to treat our opinions as fact. When we treat our opinions as facts, we impose limitations on how we interact with the world and what we declare possible. In the children's picture book *The Day the Crayons Quit*, author Drew Daywalt and illustrator Oliver Jeffers (2013) portray what can happen when we treat our opinions as the truth. The story is about a boy who opens his crayon box, only to discover the crayons are missing. Each personified crayon has written the boy a letter explaining their disappearance. Red claims it is overworked, White doesn't understand the point of being used, and Beige is having an identity crisis. The crayons assume their stories are true and use these stories to decide they will no longer collaborate with the boy.

As mentioned, when something is true, something else is not true. This is the nature of facts. When each crayon treated their opinion as a fact, other scenarios ceased to be possible. When the red crayon assumed the boy was overworking it, the possibility of red being the boy's favourite colour disappeared as it did not align with Red's truth. When White didn't see a point for its existence, the possibility of White adding value disappeared because this did not align with White's truth.

Humans are sometimes like the crayons in *The Day the Crayons Quit* (Daywalt, 2013). We don't always differentiate between what we *perceive* as true and what *is* true. Consequently, we create imagined boundaries for what is possible. If we hold as truth that someone is difficult, we assume they can't be 'not difficult'. And so, we live life as though that person is difficult. The world we create through our interactions with the individual, our self and others becomes centred on the person being difficult. However, when we realise our opinions are opinions, we create the possibility of choosing how we use them.

Time-out to practise

Consider your last conversation.

1. What verifiable facts did you state?
2. What falsehoods may have been declared?
3. What opinions did you or others express?

What is my opinion telling me about myself?

The *Cambridge Online Dictionary* defines the word 'difficult' as 'needing skill or effort' or 'not easy to deal with or understand'. The first part of the definition suggests 'difficult' is a word we use when we believe something is challenging us. It makes the opinion not so much about the situation but how we are seeing ourselves in the situation. Perhaps we feel we have gone beyond what we think we are capable of or can understand.

The second part of the definition implies that we form an opinion that someone else is difficult when we silently declare we can no longer deal with them. It could also be a sign that we have reached the limits of our resourcefulness in the current situation. The point is the person doesn't exist as difficult. We are finding them difficult to interact with at a given point in time. This interpretation creates a whole new ball game because it suggests we define others as difficult when we hold an unspoken opinion about ourselves. If 'difficult' is a sign of how we see ourselves in the current situation, the outcome no longer relies solely on the other person not being difficult. Instead, we can have input into the outcome by using the situation as an opportunity to learn more about ourselves.

If an opinion comes from how we are seeing the world, a question to ask ourselves is, *How am I seeing the world if this is the opinion I am forming?* We can then seek to understand our opinions and how they serve us, together with what sits behind us holding the opinion. According to Sieler (2003), one way to do this is to ground the opinion. Since opinions cannot be right or wrong, the grounding process does not prove an opinion right or wrong. Instead, it gives us clarity about why we hold the opinion, what standards we are using, how the opinion is useful for us, and how we choose to use the opinion.

The process of grounding an opinion begins with asking yourself five questions about the opinion in question. It is important to respond to each question with clear-cut answers and to focus on the facts, not opinions. The process below is adapted from Sieler (2003):

1. How is holding this opinion helping me?
2. For what specific areas of life am I holding this opinion?
3. What standards am I using to inform this opinion?

4. What facts support the opinion?

5. What facts are evidence against the opinion?

Once you understand what sits beneath the opinion, you can make conscious choices about how to use it. Some choices may include:

- Shifting the opinion to a more useful opinion.
- Choosing how to interact (or not interact) with the individual (if applicable).
- Shifting your standards.
- Having a conversation with someone.
- Making a request.
- Doing nothing.

It is important to note that holding an opinion is not wrong. We legitimately hold opinions to help us make sense of the world and support future action. The grounding process is not used to remove our opinions. Grounding is about understanding why we hold an opinion and how we can use it in a way that better serves us.

Time-out to practise

Use the grounding process to ground an opinion you hold.

1. What did you learn about why you are holding the opinion?

2. What did you learn about the areas of your life in which you hold the opinion?

3. How will you use the opinion in future?

Our Way of Being and opinions

Suppose we want to understand how to work with someone we assess as difficult. In that case, we can benefit from understanding what is happening in our Way of Being. The first question to ask ourselves is: what are we telling ourselves about the situation? We might tell ourselves the other person is difficult, but what else are we saying to ourselves about the situation, including what we are saying about ourselves and our ability to handle the situation?

We attach moods and emotions to our stories and opinions. When we see someone as difficult but are unaware of our moods and emotions, we reduce the options for responding. In *New Ways of Seeing*, Mark Tyrrell (2014) claims that when we are in a heightened emotional state, our thinking becomes polarised, and we see the world in a right or wrong, true or false way. Tyrrell (2014) suggests that when we do this, seeing anything outside our current thinking can be challenging, meaning we don't understand the bigger picture. This can apply when we perceive someone as difficult. If we only see that the person is difficult, we don't see that they are responding to their interpretation of our behaviour just as we are responding to our interpretation of their behaviour.

It is important to understand our moods and emotions and how they motivate us to act and influence our perception of what is really going on. When we understand our moods and emotions, we can understand and choose how we want to use them. This could include attaching new emotions to our stories and opinions wherever doing so will serve us.

Since our language, moods and emotions become a part of our body, it is always helpful to notice what is happening in our body. Where are our components of language, moods and emotions sitting? How is that helping us? What body configuration would support us in taking more useful action? Once we understand the Way of Being informing our opinions, we can choose what will support us in using our opinions to act in ways that serve us better.

Time-out to practise

Reflect on an opinion you are holding about someone.

1. What stories are you telling yourself about the person?
2. What stories are you telling yourself about yourself?
3. What moods and emotions are attached to your stories and opinion?
4. What is happening within your body?

How do I deal with a difficult person?

Tyrrell (2014) claims there is power in reframing a situation, as it offers another perspective. His view makes sense. Just as we respond to others from our Way of Being, others respond to us from their Way of Being. They interpret our behaviour and act in a way that makes sense to them based on how they are seeing the world. So, as well as understanding our own Way of Being, it helps to understand what is happening in the Way of Being of the person we see as difficult.

When dealing with someone you perceive as difficult, it helps to ask yourself:

- How might the person I see as difficult be interpreting my behaviour from their Way of Being?
- What about the other person's Way of Being is leading to behaviour I choose to interpret as difficult?
- What in their language, moods and emotions, and body are informing their actions?

According to Sieler (2003), each of us has 'concerns' or things that 'matter most to us', which influence our perceptions and actions as we interact with the world. We may or may not be aware of the presence of concerns, since they can underpin the very core of our being without us even realising. Regardless, Sieler (2003) claims that 'Humans are walking sets of concerns waiting to be taken care of' (p109), indicating that, in our interactions with others, we will interpret and respond based on how our concerns are met. An example of a concern over how we are being might be a deeply held fear about our worthiness or value. We can also have concerns that relate to our doing, such as a Chief Financial Officer being concerned about financial governance.

Regardless of whether a concern is about being or doing, we interpret and act based on how our concerns are met. So, when we react to someone by labelling them as difficult, something that matters deeply to us is not being met in that interaction, leading us to label the person as difficult.

Whenever you find yourself reacting to how you perceive another person's behaviour, it helps to understand what concerns of yours are not being met. Ask yourself:

- What is important to me in this interaction that is not being taken care of?
- Would I still like this concern to be met? If so, how can I shift my Way of Being to support the concern being met?

Just as we look for *our* concerns to be met, other people are doing the same regarding matters or concerns that are important to them. Therefore, the behaviour we interpret as difficult could be the other person's response to *their* concerns not being met. Ask yourself:

- What concerns am I not addressing for the other person?
- How can I shift my Way of Being, so I respond to their Way of Being in a way that addresses their concerns?

As an example of a concern not being met, I recall a client who found her new manager aggressive, often seeming annoyed with her. One day, the manager told my client that he felt the organisation was holding him to account for several actions without giving him the authority he needed to complete them. This made him feel as though he needed approval to make decisions that he should be able to make independently. What's more, the approval he sought was often not granted. Eventually, my client realised her manager cared deeply about the way in which people held his authority and that his concern was not being met by their organisation's leadership team.

My client became curious about how she was interacting with her manager and wondered whether anything she was doing might not be taking his need to be held in authority into account. She subsequently tailored her communication in a way that she hoped would address her manager's need to feel as though she valued and respected his authority. When my client deliberately chose how to speak to her manager, he responded by changing how he spoke to her. In this way, my client helped turn the relationship around, and they were able to work together to create more useful outcomes.

In addition to trying to understand the other person's Way of Being and what in our Way of Being is leading us to see them as difficult, it is also useful to understand what might help us to accept and work with the boundaries that their behaviour appears to be creating. Ask yourself:

- What requests might be useful?
- What declarations would help?
- What conversations are missing?
- What other action/s would be helpful?

We can't control how others behave. However, if we are prepared to understand how we are interpreting the situation, as well as placing ourselves in the shoes of the other person, it may be possible for us to change how we interact with them. When we interact in a way that considers the Way of Being of the other person, addressing their concerns, we may contribute to them changing their actions. When this happens, it may well be that we no longer see the other person as difficult.

Time-out to practise

Reflect on a conversation that may not have gone well for you.

1. What did you notice in your Way of Being?
2. What did you notice in your language, moods and emotions?
3. How did your language, moods and emotions occur in your body?
4. What concerns of yours were not met during the conversation?
5. What Way of Being might the other person have been operating from?

Shifting our self-opinions

Earlier, we learnt that our opinion of someone as difficult could come from an unconscious opinion about ourselves. When seeking to understand why we are labelling someone as difficult, it is important to understand the opinion we hold of ourselves that sits behind our opinion of the other person. For example, what judgements are we making about ourselves and our ability to deal with the situation at hand that leads us to see the other person as difficult?

When we understand the opinions we hold of ourselves, we can understand how these are affecting our ability to take action. We can then explore the Way of Being behind our self-opinions and consider which Way of Being would support us in either shifting these opinions or using them more effectively. A starting point for this might be to use the grounding process to explore our self-opinions (as well as our opinion that the other person is difficult).

Time-out to practise

Reflect on a situation where you have labelled someone as difficult.

1. What are you saying to yourself about yourself?
2. What would you like to be saying to yourself about yourself?
3. What Way of Being would support you in having this new conversation with yourself?

A Deeper Reflection

Think of a person you see as difficult. In your own words, write out your interpretation of the situation. Circle the opinions and underline the facts.

1. What opinions are you treating as facts?
2. What opinions would be helpful to explore using the grounding process?
3. How might you use the opinions in a way that serves you?
4. What Way of Being underpins your opinion of the person as difficult?
5. What concerns of yours are not being taken care of?
6. What Way of Being might the other person be operating from?
7. What concerns of the other person are not being met?
8. How could you change your Way of Being to support you in meeting the concerns of the other person during a conversation with them?
9. What Way of Being would support you in interacting with the other person's Way of Being in a useful way?
10. What conversations would be useful for you to have?
11. What Way of Being would support you in having those conversations?
12. What was happening for you as a learner while you were progressing through this chapter?

Key Points

- 'Difficult' is a label we give someone based on how we see them. It is not a property of the person being observed.

- Statements that can be evaluated as true or false are called facts if they are true and falsehoods if they are not true.

- Statements that cannot be evaluated as true or false are called opinions.

- Our standards inform our opinions.

- When we confuse facts and opinions, we live our opinions as the truth and limit the possibilities for how we use them.

- We can use the grounding process to understand why we hold an opinion and how it is helping us.

- Our Way of Being can influence what opinions we form and how we use them.

- We can use our learning about why we have formed the opinion of 'difficult', what standards we are using, and what moods and emotions we have attached to the opinion to choose how we engage with someone we are labelling as difficult.

CHAPTER 9

How do I find my voice and say what is on my mind?

The Story

As she settled in to commence her next session, Maggie gazed out the window and couldn't help but notice how much different the garden looked on a grey, rainy day.

'Where would you like to start today, Maggie?' asked Alex, interrupting her thoughts.

'Since our conversation about difficult people, I have been paying attention to the labels I give others.'

'Great! How has that been helpful?'

'I have become more conscious of how often I label people and the types of labels I apply. Examples include good, lazy, competent, supportive, useful and incompetent, although there are many others. It was interesting because I have realised how easy it is to treat these labels as the truth, which affects how I interact with the person.'

'That's a great insight, Maggie. Well done.'

'I have been exploring my opinions of others and looking at what opinions of myself might be informing those opinions. It has been a useful exercise, and I feel as though the way I have conversations has shifted somewhat.'

'In what way?'

'I'm starting to accept that my opinions exist and that they influence the actions I take. But I am also pausing to choose *how* I want to use the opinions.'

'Sounds like beneficial learning.'

'It really has been.'

'Brilliant. So, what would you like to share today?'

'I don't always speak up, whether at work, at home, with friends, or wherever. Sometimes, I say nothing, even though I know that speaking up and owning what I want to say would be more useful. I let people speak over me. Inwardly, I want to say something, but then I hesitate and choose to say nothing. This happens in any situation. Like, the other night, a friend and I went out for dinner. My friend suggested sushi. I don't like fish, and I don't like seaweed. So, sushi does not appeal to me. Yet, I said nothing, agreed with what my friend wanted and ate a sushi dinner. Needless to say, I didn't enjoy it in the slightest.'

'What happens at work?'

'Work is similar. Something may not seem right, but I don't speak up. I don't have a voice.'

'Right. What do you hope to achieve from this conversation?'

'I want to find my voice. I want to speak my thoughts, and I want to be listened to.'

'And what does finding your voice look like?'

I don't want to be too scared to say what is on my mind. I want to choose when I speak and don't speak, and I want my words to be listened to.

'Finding my voice is about speaking up and saying what is on my mind, without worrying about the outcome. I want to speak up and be heard, and I want my words to be worth listening to.'

'What is stopping you from having a voice now?'

Wow. Good question.

Maggie stared out the window. The garden appeared quiet and less vibrant than usual, a product of the bleak weather.

A long, drawn-out exhalation suggested Maggie's readiness to respond.

'I don't feel safe in speaking up.'

'Why not?'

'I'm not sure.'

'When you want to speak up and can't, how does your body respond?'

'To be honest, my body feels terrible.'

'Can you draw your attention to what is happening, and really notice what "feeling terrible" means? What do you notice?'

'My body is diminished. Reduced, kind of. As though it is shrinking.'

'Anything else?'

That isn't enough?

'My breathing is shallow and rapid. My head is looking down. My chest is concave, and my stomach and chest are tight.'

'What emotions are present?'

'I'm not sure I can name them all.'

'Perhaps explain your stories and emotions, if you can't name the emotions.'

'Fear. I fear looking silly or doing the wrong thing by whoever I am with. And what if what I say has no impact? I want to have influence and be valued. I fear not being able to do that.'

Alex waited for Maggie to continue.

'I also want to stay hidden. I am avoiding what might happen, like I am timid or shy. Anxious, even.'

'Why do you want to hide?'

'I am not sure.'

'Do you trust what you have to say?'

Another good question. And I am not sure of the answer.

Maggie took her time to respond, staring out the window and reflecting on the question.

'Most of the time, I assess that what I want to say is useful or important. Sometimes, I am uncertain about what I am saying, but most of the time, I assume my input adds value and needs to be said.'

'Then why would speaking up make you look silly?'

Silence.

'I am worried about what other people will think. Will they judge me or dislike me? Will they think I am silly?'

'Isn't their response their choice?'

'I guess so.'

'Why are you taking that choice away from them?'

That's a different perspective!

Maggie took a moment to reflect. When she spoke, she pondered over her words.

'Their choices aren't my fault. Woah, that's big!'

Alex waited for Maggie to continue.

'I get it now. I am trying to protect myself by removing choice from other people. If I don't speak, they can't reject my words. They can't judge me. I want to be respected and valued, and I am afraid of that not happening. If I don't speak up, I don't risk losing their respect or causing them to devalue me.'

'Interesting. Can I ask a question?'

'Sure.'

'If you don't speak up, do you risk *not* gaining respect or being valued?'

Wow. Another different way of seeing things.

'Oh. Yeah, I guess that makes sense.'

'What would it take for you to speak up and let others choose how they respond?'

'I don't know.'

The silence seemed to go on for several minutes. Alex spoke first.

'Maggie, if someone doesn't like what you say, what are they rejecting?'

Silence.

Wow. That hit hard. My entire body reacted to that question.

Maggie spoke, her voice quiet, 'I am seeing it as a rejection of me.'

'Tell me more.'

'If others reject what I say, then I interpret that as them rejecting me.'

'Interesting.'

'Yes, and I never saw their actions as their choice before. I assumed someone rejecting my idea meant I was wrong. It didn't occur to me that it was their choice whether to accept or like my words. They will form opinions about my words and make a choice. Their choice is their choice. I am worried about the risks for me, so I am avoiding those risks by not giving a choice to others.'

'Sounds like a huge realisation.'

'Yes, but I am not sure how to shift my Way of Being around this.'

'Would it help to consider your words as an offer?'

'What do you mean?'

'Well, when you speak up, you are offering your words to others. Or, if you like, you are offering your voice. When we make an offer to someone, they can either accept or decline the offer. So, if you considered your words or voice as an offer, do you think your story would shift from one of *you* being rejected to one of your *offer* being accepted or declined?'

Wow!

'I never thought of considering what I say as an offer.'

'We make offers when we assess someone may need our help to move a situation forward. Would you be offering your voice if you knew your words wouldn't help move the situation forward?'

'No, I wouldn't.'

Alex and Maggie sat, saying nothing, until Maggie spoke.

'This is powerful. If I offered someone a lift to work, and they declined, I wouldn't interpret that as rejection. I would assume my offer was being declined. I want this to be the same for my voice. I mean, it's the other person's choice. If I offer my voice, they can choose to accept or decline it. Not me, but my voice.'

'Is this something you would like to achieve?'

'Absolutely.'

'We spoke of the stories, moods and emotions, and body preventing you from speaking up. My interpretation is you wanted to hide. It sounded as though fear and timidity were present, and you spoke about how these emotions and moods sat in your body. Does this sound correct?'

'Yes.'

'This seems to be your Way of Being around speaking up. Your Way of Being is leading you to take the action of avoiding risk. Different ways of being make different actions available to us. My question is, what new Way of Being would support you in treating your voice as an offer and in making that offer?'

A long silence.

That question makes so much sense.

'A Way of Being that allows me to accept that people won't always like what I offer. Also, being curious about what my offer can create. Becoming curious about what is possible and wondering what my offer will achieve or create. I also wonder if considering peace as an emotion might be helpful. Just being at peace with myself and my offer.'

WHAT IF LIFE CAME WITH A USER GUIDE?

'Beautiful. So, you have suggested that peace, which is an emotion from which we tell ourselves that all is well, curiosity and wonder would be helpful. And you also seem to be reframing your stories. What body would support you to achieve this Way of Being?'

Maggie stood up, ready to practise a body to support her in offering her voice.

'When I see myself not offering my voice, my body is diminished and rigid. In this situation, I think it would be helpful to open and expand my body while also being relaxed rather than rigid.'

'How would you do that?'

'Standing taller, as though a balloon is attached to my head. By lifting my head and shoulders, I am taller.'

'And your breathing?'

'My breathing is quite shallow when I am deciding whether to speak up. It would be useful if my breathing was deeper and I could slow it down. When I move my shoulders back and open my torso, my breathing seems to deepen, making it easier to slow down my breaths.'

'Excellent. And how would the Way of Being you described allow you to give yourself permission to offer your voice?'

Maggie closed her eyes as she reflected on her new Way of Being.

'To me, being at peace and more open and accepting of others will allow me to be more open and accepting of myself. I will give myself permission to offer my voice from this Way of Being.'

'How does this differ from your Way of Being before making the shift?' asked Alex.

'I focused on protecting myself rather than on what to include in my offer. Now, with this new Way of Being, I know it has nothing to do with me and everything to do with making an offer available to the other person.'

'How does that help you?'

'Instead of worrying about what others might think, I am

focusing on what offer I can make to move things forward. I think I could really use this at work. Sometimes, something may not be working for me at work, and speaking up is the only way to change that. For example, I have been chasing someone all week for a task they promised me on Monday. I want to be calm and kind, yet there is still no outcome, and now I am under pressure. But I haven't spoken up about it. I can offer my voice to the situation, to move things forward.'

'Sounds great. So where would you like to go from here, Maggie?'

'I understand why I had difficulty speaking up and am ready to end the conversation. I became caught up in what people thought of me again. I am more empowered and ready to take part in conversations now.'

'Excellent. What declaration would you like to make today?'

Another long pause.

Breaking the silence, Maggie declared, 'I offer my voice to others from a place of dignity and self-respect.'

'Would you like to try that from the body you created earlier?'

Maggie stood up again, practising the body that she now knew would support her in offering her voice. With her head held high and a tall, straight spine, she said, 'I offer my voice to others from a place of dignity and self-respect.'

'How was that?'

'Wonderful.'

'Fantastic! I think that's a wrap for today. Well done, Maggie.'

The Learning

Way of Being and speaking up

As we have learnt, our language, moods and emotions live in our body. If we take the time to notice and listen to our body, we can find cues about what components of language, moods and emotions might be present.

When Maggie tried to find her voice and speak up, she said her body felt 'terrible'. At first, she couldn't articulate why her body felt terrible, or what that meant. However, when she focused on noticing the sensations within her body, she learnt more about finding her voice and why doing so seemed difficult.

The practice of noticing what is happening within our body is what Alan Fogel (2021) refers to in *Restorative embodiment and resilience: A guide to disrupt habits, create inner peace, deepen relationships, and feel greater presence* as 'embodied self-awareness'. He proposes this type of awareness can take one of two forms:

- We can notice what we are feeling in our body.
- We can notice our thoughts about ourselves.

Fogel (2021) says embodied self-awareness helps our mental and physical wellbeing, claiming a lack of this awareness can impair our wellbeing. Our language, moods and emotions, and body are all key parts of both our wellbeing and our Way of Being. This implies that embodied self-awareness not only affects our wellbeing but can also shift our Way of Being.

Finding our voice is about noticing what is happening within our body, then using that awareness to understand how our Way of Being is limiting us and what Way of Being might serve us better.

Maggie focused on her body to understand what the 'terrible' feeling was saying to her. Signs such as a smaller posture, concave chest and dropped head gave clues about her stories and emotions and showed Maggie she wanted to stay hidden and closed off to people. These clues alerted her to emotions such as fear and timidity.

Maggie also mentioned she saw risks in speaking up, suggesting a link to trust, since trust is a risk assessment. Chapter 6 provided more detail around trust, together with emotions such as doubt, prudence and faith, all of which may be useful in exploring how to speak up.

Our body is home to our moods and emotions, which move us to action based on how we view the world. Some moods and emotions encourage us to want to find our voice and speak up. Others will do the opposite and move us towards not wanting to speak up. Noticing the emotions we experience, why they are present, and what action they are moving us towards helps us find and use our voice.

Time-out to practise

Bring your attention to your body, focusing first on your breathing, then slowly moving to other parts of your body. What do you notice?

1. How is your breathing?
2. What sensations do you notice?
3. Where is your body tense?
4. Where is your body relaxed?
5. How are your limbs, shoulders and head positioned?
6. What is the position of your spine?
7. What moods and emotions are present?
8. What stories are present?

Self-opinions and finding our voice

Can our negative self-opinions lead us to struggle when it comes to finding our voice? As we progress through life, we make sense of our world by forming opinions of ourselves and others. These opinions sometimes become ingrained, sitting in the background, informing how we are being in life. When these ingrained opinions are about ourselves, they can form a key part of who we are, becoming what Sieler (2003) refers to as 'core self-assessments'.

Sieler (2003) claims negative core self-assessments can play over and over in the background of our existence.

Similarly, Brenner (2018) claims that our negative self-view can become part of our belief system. This can drive our stories of worthiness and our choices in life. One of the key questions to support us in finding our voice is: *What am I saying to myself about myself?* When we understand our self-opinions and the identity they are creating, we can then understand the Way of Being behind them. This enables us to understand the Way of Being that would help us shift these opinions.

Opinions gain authority from the listener, not from being spoken. This means when we are listening to our own opinions, we don't have to give them authority. We can choose not to listen to our self-opinions, and we can also choose not to let them influence us. One way of deciding what authority to give an opinion is to use the grounding process offered in Chapter 8.

In *On My Own Side: Transform Self-Criticism and Doubt Into Permanent Self-Worth and Confidence,* Dr Aziz Gazipura (2019) suggests we can shift our unhelpful views of ourselves by becoming 'our own best friend'. When we treat ourselves as we would a best friend, offering kindness and warmth to ourselves and pausing our judgements to become curious about our Way of Being, we can learn to make choices about how we want to be and what we want to do. Gazipura (2019) suggests the approach of being our own best friend is more useful than simply shifting our self-talk. His suggestion makes sense since becoming our own best friend requires a shift in our Way of Being. If we only shift the 'doing' around our self-talk, this may not be sustainable since old ways of being would still be informing our self-talk. So how do we become our own best friend? One of the first steps is to ask ourselves how we would treat a friend in the same situation. Then we could explore the Way of Being that would support us in treating ourselves the same way.

Time-out to practise

Find a quiet place where you can tune into your inner thoughts and chatter.

1. What are you saying to yourself about yourself and, in particular, about being able to speak up or not speak up?
2. What Way of Being would help you change these stories about yourself?
3. What Way of Being would help you become your own best friend?
4. What step will you take towards becoming your own best friend?

Why worry about what other people think?

To some degree, society relies on us being mindful of what others think. Without this collective mindfulness, we would struggle to maintain order because we wouldn't have the resulting shame to keep us in check. However, when worrying about what others think goes beyond maintaining order and becomes a part of us, it can limit our Way of Being and how we take action. Thinking we must be how others expect us to be can lead us to place unhelpful boundaries and standards on ourselves.

In *What Will People Think? How to be Confident in Yourself and Stop Worrying About What People Think*, Roma Sharma (2020) offers that the greater the regard we have for someone, the greater the value we place on their opinions. This suggests how we are seeing someone, and perhaps even how we are seeing ourselves, can influence the importance we place on what a person may think. Our regard for others is part of our Way of Being and comes from our past learning, our culture, our values, and our experience of life.

Our Way of Being is the point from which we view the world, influencing both our interpretation of the world and the actions we take. This means our Way of Being will inform the value we place on the thoughts of others while also informing how we use these opinions and thoughts. Understanding why we worry about what others think requires us to understand how we are seeing the world. What importance are we placing on the individual's opinion, and why? What in our Way of Being has us labelling their opinion as important?

The following questions may help us understand the meaning we are giving to the opinions of others and why that meaning is important to us:

- What am I saying to myself about the worthiness of others in this situation?
- What am I saying to myself about my worthiness in this situation?
- What value am I placing on others and their opinions in this situation?
- What value am I placing on myself and my opinions in this situation?
- What moods and emotions am I attaching to the situation?
- What is happening in my body during my experience of this situation?

When we realise what in our Way of Being is placing importance on other people's opinions, we can seek to understand what permission we are giving to these opinions. Opinions cannot affect us without our permission. How do we change our Way of Being to shift the permission we are giving to the opinion? You can explore this further using the grounding process discussed in Chapter 8.

Understanding our Way of Being will help us make deliberate choices about how we use the opinions of ourselves and others. What Way of Being will support us in choosing how we use the opinions of others? For example, a Way of Being centred around curiosity may be helpful; however, it will depend on what we find useful in the situation we are experiencing.

An emotion that can be helpful when we want to make our own choices and own our own outcomes is dignity. From a place of dignity, our story becomes 'I decide' or 'I choose'. Dignity is the emotion where we take care of our own legitimacy and step into our worthiness. When we use dignity to guide us through other people's opinions, we are stepping into our worthiness and declaring that we will choose what happens next. We won't allow the opinion to make that choice for us. Metaphorically speaking, it is engaging our 'I choose' shield.

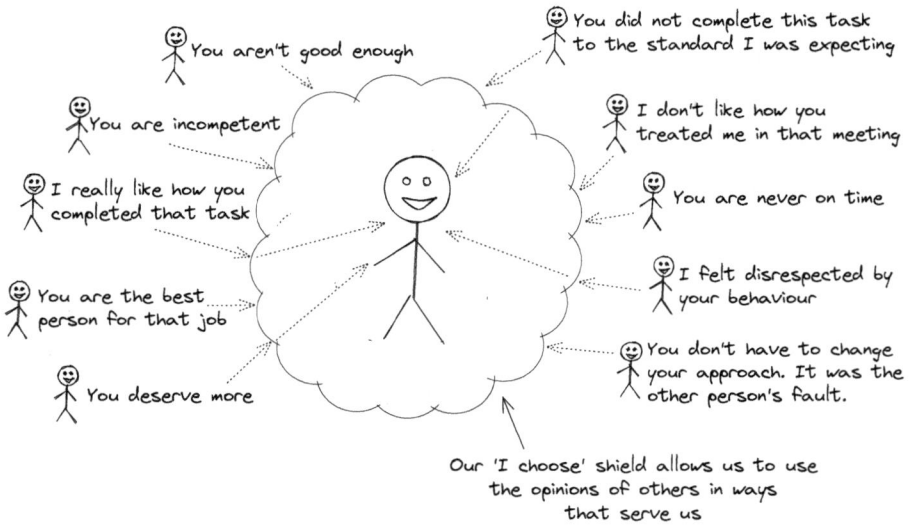

Figure 12: *Our 'I choose' shield can help us choose if and how the opinions of others will affect us*

Figure 12 shows how we can use dignity to create our 'I choose' shield, allowing us to make a deliberate choice about how to use opinions offered to us by others. We can choose how each opinion is likely to help us and how we want to use it, including whether we want to let it through our 'I choose' shield or deal with it in another way. This doesn't mean ignoring the opinions we think are bad and giving credence to the opinions we think are good. Sometimes, what we think is good won't serve us, and what we think is bad might serve us. The 'I choose' shield enables us to make a deliberate choice about what is likely to serve us or not serve us in each moment.

Time-out to practise

Recall some opinions that others have offered you.

1. What level of importance did you place on these opinions?
2. What permission did you give to the opinions?
3. What Way of Being would have supported you in engaging your 'I choose' shield so you could have chosen how to respond to these opinions?

What if you considered your voice as an offer to others?

Maggie said she hesitated to speak up because she was worried about what other people might think of her. She was afraid of being rejected. Alex suggested that while Maggie could offer her thoughts, it was up to other people to choose how they responded, implying that perhaps Maggie was taking this choice away from others when she didn't speak up. This leads to the idea of our voice being an offer for others to either accept or decline.

In improvisational theatre, actors speak and respond to lines without any prior planning, creating an unscripted show that entertains the audience through complete randomness. Without a script, each actor's response becomes an important building block for whatever eventually unfolds. The scene will only move forward when the actors offer each other a building block.

Max Dickins (2020) supports this idea in *Improvise!: Use the secrets of improv to achieve extraordinary results at work*, where he claims each actor's response is an offer from one actor to another, with an offer being defined as '[...] any piece of information that is added to the scene'. The show will only move forward if the scene is added to, that is, if the actors keep giving and receiving offers. Each actor must accept the offered line without judgement and build on it before making an offer of their own. In effect, actors in an improvisational theatre show have made an unspoken commitment that they will continue to offer their voices for the duration of the show. This commitment makes their interaction a success and contributes to comedy gold.

Like actors in improvisational theatre, when we choose to speak up, our voice becomes an offer to others. Whether others accept our voice or build on it is their choice and out of our control. An unaccepted offer does not mean the offer is wrong or we are not enough. It simply means someone chose not to accept or build on the offer. Nothing more. If an improv actor refused to respond to an offer, the scene would not move forward, creating the risk of a failed collaboration. Similarly, refusing to offer our voice to others could result in our interactions missing an opportunity to move forward, risking the creation of useful outcomes. We can create new possibilities when we offer our voice to others. It is up to the recipient of our offer to choose whether to accept and expand on those possibilities.

Maggie and Alex were borrowing ideas from improvisational theatre when they spoke of Maggie seeing her voice as an offer. Whether people accept or decline Maggie's offer is their choice, based on how they are interpreting the world. It is not a reflection on Maggie or what she has to say. It is only a reflection on how others may be interpreting what Maggie has offered.

Improvisational theatre is less effective if the actors refuse to make or accept offers or don't remain present to the improv. Becoming anxious about their performance or judgemental about the lines offered shifts the focus to themselves and how they are feeling, making them less present to the improv and the performance they are trying to create. Consequently, the Way of Being of an improv artist is such that it requires their language, moods and emotions, and body to support accepting and building on offers. Perhaps this could include acceptance that the offers of other actors are the boundaries within which everyone operates and curiosity about how they can build on the offer and move the scene forward.

Understanding how the Way of Being of an improv actor supports their performance can provide an insight into how our Way of Being may support us in offering our voice to others. For example, a Way of Being caught in anxiety about what others might think or whether what we have to say is good enough may not be conducive to moving our interactions forward. In this situation, it is helpful to ask ourselves, *What Way of Being would support me in making my voice an offer to others?*

Time-out to practise

1. What Way of Being would support you in viewing your voice as an offer to others?
2. What Way of Being would support you in making that offer—that is, in speaking up?

How to put yourself in the shoes of others when speaking up

Sieler (2007) and Kegan and Lahey (2001) suggest we each have fundamental matters or concerns that are important to us. When we engage in a conversation, we listen to ensure the matters important to us are being considered by the other person/people involved. So, when conversing with others, it is important to speak to the concerns of the listener, to put ourselves in their shoes. The listener creates meaning from how they interpret our spoken words. Their interpretations relate to how well they believe their concerns are being met. If, for example, it is important to someone that they are valued, their interpretations will depend on whether they see this need being met.

When we put ourselves in the shoes of those we are speaking to, we can tailor the offer of our voice to speak to what is important to them. Let's say you want to speak up to a manager about the quality of their team's work. Putting yourself in the manager's shoes will help you understand how the manager may be viewing the situation. Once you understand the manager's perspective, you can adapt your words to ensure they take the manager's concerns into account. Maybe the team's standard of work has dropped because they are under-resourced. In this case, you could raise concerns about the quality of the team's output while also offering to assist with a recruitment process. Or perhaps some team members lack certain skills required for the project they are working on. In that case, you could offer to help find a suitable training program for them. The manager is still presented with a problem, but it is done in a way that shows their challenges are being heard.

Time-out to practise

1. What Way of Being would support you in placing yourself in someone else's shoes?
2. How would you use this new understanding of someone else's perspective to ensure you speak to their concerns when offering your voice?

WHAT IF LIFE CAME WITH A USER GUIDE?

A Deeper Reflection

Think of a situation in which you felt unable to find your voice and imagine you are in that situation now.

1. When you try to speak up, what is happening within your Way of Being?
2. What stories and opinions are present?
3. How can you use your 'I choose' shield to use the opinions of yourself and others in ways that serve you?
4. What moods and emotions are present?
5. What would it take to consider your voice as an offer?
6. How can you put yourself in the shoes of your listeners?
7. What changes would you make to the voice you offer after being able to understand the perspective of your listeners?
8. What Way of Being will support you in speaking up?
9. How would you shift to that new Way of Being?
10. What was happening for you as a learner while you were progressing through this chapter?

Key Points

- Our Way of Being will either support us in speaking up or not support us in speaking up.
- Our stories and self-opinions can limit us in finding our voice.
- We can choose what permission we give to our opinions of ourselves and to other people's opinions of us.
- Our 'I choose' shield enables us to hold ourselves as legitimate and use opinions to serve us.
- Our voice is an offer for others to accept or deny.
- We can put ourselves in the shoes of others to understand how to use our voice in a way that encourages others to listen and be open to what we have to say.

CHAPTER 10

How do I have a conversation that I am not looking forward to having?

The Story

'Hi Maggie! How are you?' Alex asked.

'Great, thanks! I have been practising speaking up in conversations and it has really helped. I love that whole making-an-offer-of-my-voice thing!'

'Wonderful to hear.'

'I mean, sometimes I still hesitate, but I can usually work through it when I realise what I'm doing.'

'Fantastic.'

Maggie's smile showed she thought so too.

'What are we chatting about today?' Alex asked.

'There is a conversation that I would like to have with someone, and I know it is going to be difficult. I would like to use today to figure out how to have a difficult conversation.'

'What do you mean by a difficult conversation?'

Isn't it just a conversation that is difficult?

Maggie considered her words.

'A difficult conversation is one where the topic is difficult. It's a conversation that could cause angst for the other person and me. I don't know how they will react. And if they don't see my point of view, the conversation will end in an argument.'

'How do you know?'

'I just do.'

'Okay. So, why is the conversation going to be difficult?'

'We both have different views, so the other person will most likely react, and the conversation will become emotional.'

'Have you tried to have this conversation before?'

'No. To be honest, I have been putting it off.'

'Do you mind if I clarify what I am hearing?'

'Sure. Go for it.'

'I think what I am hearing is that you want to have a conversation with someone. You haven't tried to have this conversation before, but you are expecting it to be difficult because your opinions differ, and emotions will be high. Did I understand correctly?'

'Yes.'

'I'm curious. Does the conversation have to be difficult?'

'Well, I am expecting it to be difficult.'

'Does it have to be?'

Another one of those questions I don't know how to answer.

'I guess I think it has to be difficult because that's what I am expecting.'

'What would help you to see the conversation as something different?'

'What else can I see it as?'

Alex chuckled. 'I was hoping *you* might tell me that.'

'Oops. Sorry, I've got nothing.'

'Maggie, can you tell me what emotion you have attached to your opinions of this conversation?'

With her gaze fixed on the floor, Maggie slowly exhaled. Alex, as always, held the silence until she was ready to speak.

Finally, Maggie looked up and said, 'I am certain it is dread.'

'Tell me more about dread.'

'Well, I want to avoid the conversation. I don't want to be there because I am not sure I can deal with it.'

'Dread helps us avoid what we fear. What harm do you think is likely to come from the conversation? Is there something that you are fearing?'

Alex sure knows how to ask questions that get to the crux of a matter!

'I fear ruining the relationship with this person. I don't want to hurt them, and I don't want them to dislike me or think I am being difficult.'

Alex nodded.

'So, you fear ruining your relationship with the person, and you don't want to hurt them or have them dislike you or think you are difficult?' he confirmed.

'Yes.'

'Okay, so I understand what you are afraid of and that certain things are out of your control. But is there anything you *do* have control over in that situation?'

Ah, we are back to that one again...

Maggie's gaze shifted outward to the garden and settled on the birdbath as she collected her thoughts.

'I can't directly control any of it, Alex. I can only influence it by managing how I am being in the conversation. But I can't control it.'

'Are you able to tell me more?'

'Well, I can control my Way of Being to a certain degree, which could influence how others respond to me. But I have no control over whether they are going to like me or think that I am difficult.'

'So, what does that mean for you in terms of moving forward with this?'

'I think it means my Way of Being in the conversation is going to be important.'

'Okay. Do you mind if I loop back to some points you made earlier?'

'Please do.'

'These may not be your exact words, so apologies if I don't repeat what you said verbatim. I think you said you know the conversation will be difficult, and you have differing opinions, which could result in an argument. Is that your understanding of what you said?'

'Yes.'

'Why can't the conversation simply be a conversation? Why does it have to be difficult? Why does it have to be anything?'

Silence.

Alex, you are a genius.

'Oh wow. The conversation doesn't have to be difficult. It doesn't have to be anything! It is my Way of Being about this conversation that has me seeing it as difficult.'

'What would it take to see it as a conversation? No judgement, just a conversation that will be whatever it will be?'

'I am anxious about how it will go. However, I could shift that anxiety. Perhaps some acceptance that our opinions most likely differ. I am also wondering whether it might be helpful for me to be curious about how the conversation will go and compassionate towards the other person.'

'How will those emotions help?'

'The other person will respond to my Way of Being. If I can come from a place of compassion and curiosity, they may feel supported rather than attacked or wrong.'

'And what would take care of *you* in the conversation?'

'Good question.'

Alex waited while Maggie took a deep breath in and slowly exhaled.

'Accepting my opinion as legitimate, and accepting it is legitimate to choose to voice my opinion. I am not wrong for having this conversation. I am holding myself and the other person to account for our actions. Also, I think some courage and dignity. Courage will help me move forward and have the conversation. Dignity will allow me to choose how I am being.'

Alex allowed an extended pause to linger before he continued.

'I wonder if I can offer a thought. My thought may not be relevant, but I am curious about something.'

'Sure.'

'I am wondering whether trust might also help you in this conversation?'

'Wow, that's a good point. I think it could be useful.'

'How would trust help you?'

'I think it would be useful to create a space for trust in the conversation, and I am wondering what Way of Being will help me communicate in a way that builds and maintains trust with the other person.'

Alex remained silent, allowing Maggie to reflect further.

She finally broke the silence. 'I think it would be useful for me to operate from compassion for the other person and perhaps curiosity about where the conversation could go. To help with curiosity, I could ask myself how the conversation might go. I could also be curious about how I can walk beside the person in the conversation, which I think would help me to be compassionate. To build trust, I would want to be authentic, and I think curiosity and compassion would help me to achieve authenticity.'

'What a great realisation! What body would support this compassionate and curious Way of Being?'

Maggie quietly reflected on Alex's question before responding with, 'An open torso, lifted shoulders and a centred spine. I would want my body to feel grounded. Straight, but not stiff.'

Maggie spent a minute or so practising the newly discovered body configuration.

'Is there anything else that might be useful?'

'Yes. It would be helpful to have trust in myself.'

'Great!'

'To be honest, I never thought of trust, so thank you for sharing that with me.'

'No problem, Maggie. What will having trust in yourself look like?'

'I want to feel competent, so I think that is about being prepared for the conversation, including understanding how the other person might be feeling. I want to be sincere, both in how I interact with the other person and in the way I deliver my message. I want to be reliable, and I want to be engaged. So, in this case, I think all components of trust are important to me. I will assess whether I meet these components prior to the conversation. I can do that by preparing for some items being discussed and understanding my Way of Being and what is likely to be important to the other person.'

'Would you like to discuss trust further?'

'Actually, I think I feel comfortable with it, thank you.'

'So where are you at?'

'I think I am ready to stop. I am comfortable that I can use what I have learnt to create a Way of Being that will serve me. I would like to explore the body of this Way of Being, but I'd like to do that at home. I think the important point for me is understanding that this conversation doesn't have to be difficult. It doesn't have to be anything but a conversation. Also, realising that I can't control what happens, only who I am being.'

'Would you like to make a declaration?'

'I am a courageous and compassionate communicator who trusts myself to deliver important messages with honesty and authenticity.'

The Learning

What is a difficult conversation?

Fair Work Australia describes a difficult conversation as follows[3]:

'In the workplace, a difficult conversation is one in which you have to manage emotions and information in a sensitive way to deal with a workplace issue.

A difficult conversation may involve:

- topics you don't want to talk about
- situations where you're not sure what to say
- conflicting opinions
- circumstances where the outcome is uncertain
- discussions which make you feel uncomfortable.'

Although specific to the workplace, this definition can apply to any situation, suggesting a difficult conversation is one where circumstances may involve uncertainty, discomfort or conflict.

We may perceive conversations as difficult, but it is our labels that make them difficult. We form an opinion of how the conversation will go and let the opinion become our truth. This 'truth' creates the conversation as difficult. Consider anchovies, for example. Some people label anchovies as tasty. Others label them as awful. The truth is anchovies are anchovies. They can't be both tasty and awful. Yet, we live our experience of them as tasty or awful based on the label we give them. The same applies to conversations. A conversation is not difficult until we label it as difficult.

---

3 'A manager's guide to difficult conversations in the workplace'. (Accessed 4 June, 2023). *Fair Work Australia.* https://www.fairwork.gov.au/sites/default/files/migration/712/managers-guide-to-difficult-conversations-in-the-workplace.pdf

Maggie declared her removal of the label of 'difficult' from her conversation. This shifted her focus from the label to the actual conversation. It is important to note that although Maggie decided the label would not help her, it is not wrong to label a conversation as difficult (or anything else for that matter). In fact, sometimes, giving something a label might be helpful. The aim is to ensure our labels serve us.

Time-out to practise

Reflect on a recent difficult conversation.

1. What led you to label the conversation as difficult?
2. How did labelling the conversation as difficult help or hinder you?
3. What labels would have been more helpful in that conversation?

Why is the conversation necessary?

A difficult conversation addresses a specific issue. The intention is to take care of all parties and move the situation forward. In *Taking Conversations from Difficult to Doable,* Lynne Cunningham (2016) suggests our primary goal should be to help the other person. Most importantly, we do not want to cause harm.

To ensure we don't create harm, we must understand why we need the conversation. Do we want to move the situation forward, or is there a different agenda? We need to be clear about this since our purpose will inform our Way of Being in the conversation. Asking ourselves the following question can help us figure out why the conversation is necessary: *For the sake of what am I having this conversation?*

Imagine you feel the need to have a conversation with a close friend about their partner because of something they have done that has broken your trust in them. In that case, ask yourself, *For the sake of what am I holding this conversation with my friend to tell them I don't trust their partner? Will the conversation help my friend move forward, or will it cause more harm than good?* Your answers to these questions will provide clarity.

For any conversation we perceive as difficult, if we discover our intention is to move a situation forward, the conversation may be helpful. If our motive is to cause harm, on the other hand, we should rethink or reframe the conversation.

Time-out to practise

Reflect on a difficult conversation you would like to hold in the future.

1. For the sake of what do you want to hold the conversation?
2. How will the conversation move the situation forward?
3. What other agendas are present?

Way of Being and difficult conversations

Our Way of Being influences our ability to declare when a conversation is needed and influences how we take part in the conversation. Maggie noticed fear and dread present in her Way of Being. Fear and dread incline us towards avoidance, which is why Maggie's Way of Being led her to want to avoid her difficult conversation. When we avoid a conversation, we create what Brothers (2005) calls a 'missing conversation'. A missing conversation can't facilitate progress because it doesn't exist. If we want to move things forward, these conversations must exist. The first step is to notice our Way of Being and the shifts needed to help us have the conversation.

Once we declare the conversation, our focus needs to shift to how we take part in it. For example, it is not uncommon to approach a difficult conversation with some fear. However, given fear is about keeping us safe, if we work from fear, we may self-protect and shift the focus to ourselves, which doesn't always help us achieve effective outcomes. The key is choosing a Way of Being that will serve the conversation and being aware of how to shift to and support our Way of Being during the conversation. The ultimate aim is to hold all parties as legitimate, which means considering the Way of Being of all members in the conversation and speaking to those ways of being as much as we can.

Time-out to practise

Imagine you are about to take part in a difficult conversation.

1. What Way of Being would help you proceed with the conversation?
2. What Way of Being would help you hold yourself and others as legitimate in the conversation?
3. How would you support your Way of Being throughout the conversation?

Creating a space of trust in a difficult conversation

Maggie wanted to create a space of trust to support the other person in being both trusted and able to trust. In *Dancing with Change: Cultivating Healthy Organisations*, Eric Lynn (2020) describes a 'trust space' as a place where we feel free to be ourselves, experiencing safety, support, protection and acceptance regardless of what is said in the conversation. He further claims that one of the paradoxes of the trust space is that, while it is very real for the person experiencing it, it is only a sense or a feeling. This makes a trust space something that sits within an individual because it is how an individual is feeling in that space and in that moment.

Lynn's (2020) view aligns with Solomon and Flores (2001), who suggest trusting depends on the Way of Being of the person who is choosing to trust, not on any properties of the person being trusted. Whether others trust us will depend on the opinions they form when they observe our Way of Being from their Way of Being.

We may hold ourselves as trustworthy, yet the other person will only see us that way if they interpret us as trustworthy. Trust is more about how the other person is experiencing us in the world than about our qualities. We can influence someone else's assessment of trust in us, but we cannot control their assessments. While we can have the intention of creating a space of trust, we can only control our own Way of Being and actions; we cannot control the interpretations of others.

One way of taking care of others in our conversations and contributing to creating a space of trust is to speak to what is important to them. Each of us has matters we regard as important. These important matters may be part of our being, such as needing to be good enough, or part of our doing, such as making sure the front door is locked when we leave the house. Kegan and Lahey (2001) refer to the matters that are important to us as 'concerns'.

When we listen in conversations, we are listening to take care of our concerns. The lens created by our concerns influences our interpretations of the world. We respond to situations based on whether our concerns are met. If our concerns are not met, meaning can be lost, causing misunderstandings, a lack of trust and conflict.

When we speak, we speak from our personal concerns. Because we are speaking from our own concerns to someone who is listening from the perspective of their concerns, we may inadvertently neglect to address the concerns of others. To avoid misunderstanding, we should aim to hold the concerns of everyone in a conversation as legitimate.

We may not know what is important to others, but we can try to put ourselves in the other person's shoes to assess what might be important to them. We can then create a Way of Being to support us in speaking to those concerns. For example, suppose we put ourselves in the shoes of someone who is hearing they no longer have a job. In that case, we may assess their concerns as being able to survive financially, maintaining their dignity and being heard. Consider what Way of Being would support us in speaking to these concerns during the conversation.

Time-out to practise

Consider how you would create a space of trust during a difficult conversation.

1. What Way of Being would support you?
2. How would you gain an understanding of what might be important to others in the conversation?
3. How would you speak to those important matters (concerns) during the conversation?

How to prepare for a difficult conversation

Difficult conversations happen because we want to move a situation forward in a way that helps ourselves and others. When getting ready to have a difficult conversation, it is important to start by preparing our Way of Being since our Way of Being creates our actions. We may know what we want to do in the conversation, but if our being does not support that doing, we may not achieve a useful outcome.

When we prepare our Way of Being, we seek to understand how we will use and embody our language, moods and emotions to create the outcome we would like to achieve. The following can be useful in preparing for a difficult conversation:

- **Determine the facts versus your opinions**

When presenting feedback to others, it is important to be clear on what is fact and what is your opinion. For example, 'You are never in the office when I need you' is an opinion about a person's availability. A fact might be, 'Four times this week when I wanted your help, you were not in the office.' How we use our facts and opinions can make a difference in our interactions.

When we treat our opinions as the truth, we place limitations on how we see and interact with people. When we push this 'truth' onto others, we force our truth to exist with their view of the world without considering what their truth may be. We are removing the possibility of the other person having a different view and imposing our opinion on them. Perhaps this is useful. Perhaps it is not. However, if we understand the facts and opinions, we can decide how we use each. We can also be open to the possibility of the other person offering us a different perspective. What we see as someone who is never in the office could be someone who is struggling with a challenging situation at home, someone who is investing significant time in managing an unhappy customer, or something else. It may not simply be that the person is never in the office.

- **Consider what Way of Being will support you and others in the conversation**

What language, moods and emotions will be helpful for you, and how will you embody them? For example, if you are anxious about a difficult conversation, you might focus on self-protection and how you are feeling, making it challenging to be present for the other person. In this case, consider how you could be, other than anxious, that would support you and others more effectively during the conversation. One approach might be a Way of Being centred on curiosity, service or something similar.

- **Ask yourself: *what body will support my Way of Being?***

Although body is part of our Way of Being, it is worth mentioning as a separate point here to highlight how important it is to identify the body we want to support our language, moods and emotions. When preparing for a difficult conversation, consider how your body will contribute to your Way of Being. One way to explore the body that will serve you is to notice where the language, moods and emotions you want to operate from sit within your body and then adjust your body accordingly.

After exploring your body as part of your Way of Being, the next step is to practise elements of the conversation from that body so you can understand how your body is supporting the conversation. Then, just before you begin the actual conversation, body movements such as simple stretches, shoulder and neck exercises, or any other movement you find useful can help shift your body into your chosen Way of Being.

- **Consider what will help you contribute to a space of trust**

We have learnt that a space of trust is an individual feeling. We can contribute to a space of trust for others, but whether the other person perceives it as a space of trust will depend on their own interpretation. Placing yourself in the other person's shoes, what actions will support you in contributing to a space of trust for that individual? What Way of Being will enable you to take those actions? This will require you to consider what the other person might be feeling and what matters might be important to them.

For example, let's say you are in a difficult conversation with someone, and you interpret that feeling valued matters more to them than anything else. In this case, what Way of Being would support you in taking actions in the conversation that may contribute to the person feeling valued and assessing that you have created a space of trust for them? Understanding what will help you experience a space of trust in the conversation is equally important. Ask yourself, *What Way of Being will support me in holding myself as legitimate, taking care of matters that are important to me and helping me feel as though a space of trust exists?* Note that some of this will depend on how you interpret the other person's behaviour as the conversation progresses. So, the next question to ask yourself is, *What Way of Being will help me remain curious about how I might be interpreting their behaviour?*

Time-out to practise

Think about a difficult conversation you would like to have.

1. What facts will you be presenting in the conversation?
2. What opinions will you be presenting?
3. What might be important to the other person?
4. What is important to you?
5. How will you present the facts and your opinions in a way that takes care of both the other person and you?
6. What Way of Being will support you in achieving the above?

A Deeper Reflection

Consider the same or another difficult conversation you would like to have:

1. For the sake of what is the conversation necessary?
2. What outcome are you trying to achieve?
3. What Way of Being will support you in having the conversation?
4. Write down your thoughts about the conversation, including why it should happen, why you see it as difficult, and how you are seeing the other person.

   a. What facts and opinions are present?

   b. How will you use this information in the conversation?

5. What is important to take care of in the conversation?

   a. What do you assess as important to the other person?

   b. How will you take care of those concerns?

   c. What is important to you and how will you take care of your concerns?

6. What will support you in creating a space of trust during the conversation?
7. How will you keep track of your Way of Being during the conversation?
8. What was happening for you as a learner while you were progressing through this chapter?

Key Points

- A difficult conversation is one where we perceive there will be uncertainty, discomfort or conflict.
- A conversation is a conversation until we label it as difficult.
- Our Way of Being can affect our approach to difficult conversations.
- It is important to create a space of trust in a difficult conversation.
- Everyone has concerns to be taken care of. We listen and speak from our concerns but also need to be mindful of the concerns of others in a difficult conversation.
- It helps to speak to the concerns of the others involved in the conversation and understand what may be happening in their Way of Being.

CHAPTER 11

A six-step model for navigating life

Model Overview

Our past learning creates the foundation from which we communicate with ourselves and others as we progress through life. This foundation is our Way of Being, the place from which we observe and take action in the world. Throughout life, most of us don't learn to become aware of and explore our Way of Being, which means we seldom realise what is sitting behind our behaviours. Instead, we assume we are seeing the world as it is, forming judgements about the behaviour of ourselves and others, and accepting those judgements as 'the truth' about how the world exists when they are really our own personal truths.

The six-step model described in this final chapter offers a pathway to create change and support us as we navigate everyday life.

The model assumes:

- We operate from a Way of Being in any given moment. This Way of Being comprises what is happening for us in our language, moods and emotions, and body and is the place from which we observe and take action in the world.

- No one is at fault for any interaction. Rather, everyone is responding from their Way of Being, and the combination of those responses sometimes produces outcomes that may not be useful.

- Our Way of Being is a source of learning. We can explore the Way of Being behind our actions and behaviours and use this learning to shift to more resourceful ways of being.

- Curiosity and reflection can show us what new paths are possible.

Maggie and Alex used a six-step model to help Maggie navigate her everyday life challenges. The six steps in the model are:

1. Declare that there is an issue.
2. Seek to understand the issue.
3. Explore possible ways forward.
4. Declare a way forward.
5. Take action.
6. Reflect on the results.

If we look closely at the conversations between Maggie and Alex, we can see how they followed these steps:

1. At the beginning of each conversation, Maggie would declare what she wanted to change.
2. Through asking questions, Maggie and Alex gained clarity about the issue or change Maggie had raised.
3. Further questioning allowed Maggie and Alex to determine what was possible. This included understanding what change Maggie might make and what would help her make that change.
4. After exploring the possibilities, Maggie would choose and declare a new way forward. By expressing a new way forward, she brought it into existence so she could be held to account.
5. Following the coaching conversation, Maggie would use her learning from the exchange to take action.
6. Maggie would then reflect on what had been useful and what she could do differently, reporting on this at the next coaching conversation.

Although it might be easy to assume these six steps alone created new outcomes for Maggie, they are only part of the overall model. Our Way of Being underpins every action we take, and so, as Figure 13 shows, the following six-step model is underpinned by our Way of Being, comprising our language, moods and emotions, and body.

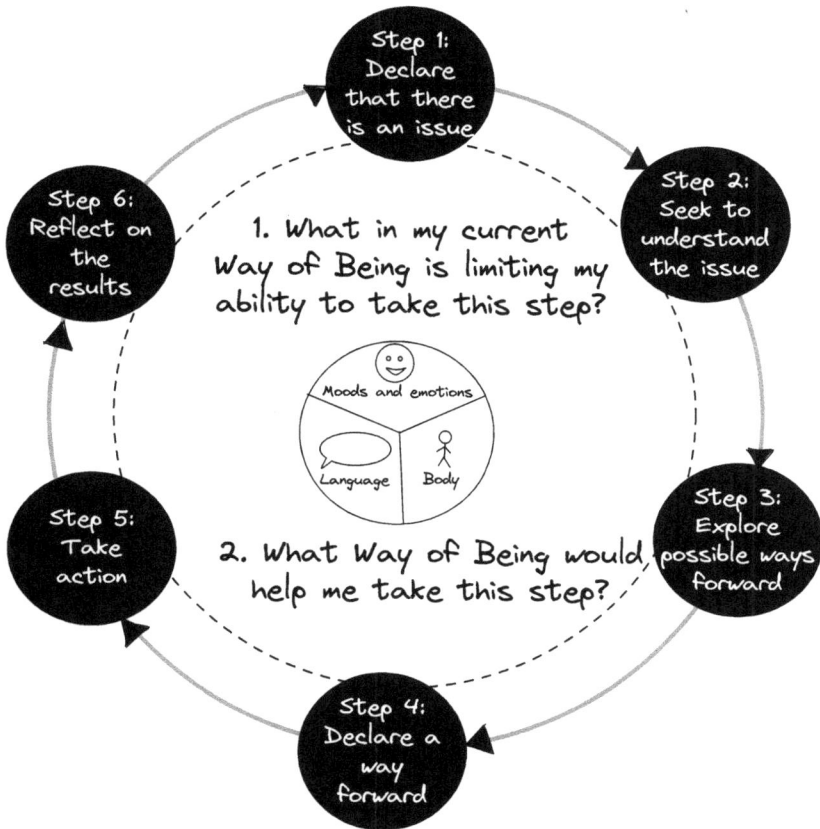

Figure 13: *A six-step model for navigating life*

When we are trying to create change to help us navigate life, there are two key questions to ask ourselves:

1. What, in my current Way of Being, is limiting my ability to take this step?
2. What new Way of Being will help me take this step?

We can ask these questions for each step of the model, but also for the bigger picture change we are trying to create.

Now let's explore the model in more detail and consider how to apply it in everyday life.

Step 1: Declare that there is an issue

As we progress through life, we are how we are being and do what we are doing, often without realising what we are creating in life. We operate on autopilot, making silent choices that are not visible to us.

Before we can take action to change a situation, we must be aware of the need to change and accept that we want things to be different. After all, we can't change what we are not aware of. So, the first step in the model is: *Declare that there is an issue.*

As Figure 14 shows, when we declare that there is an issue, we are drawing a line in the sand between where life is now and where we want it to be. In so doing, we announce that we no longer want to follow Path X and will instead follow Path Y. Importantly, we are declaring that we are prepared to take the next step.

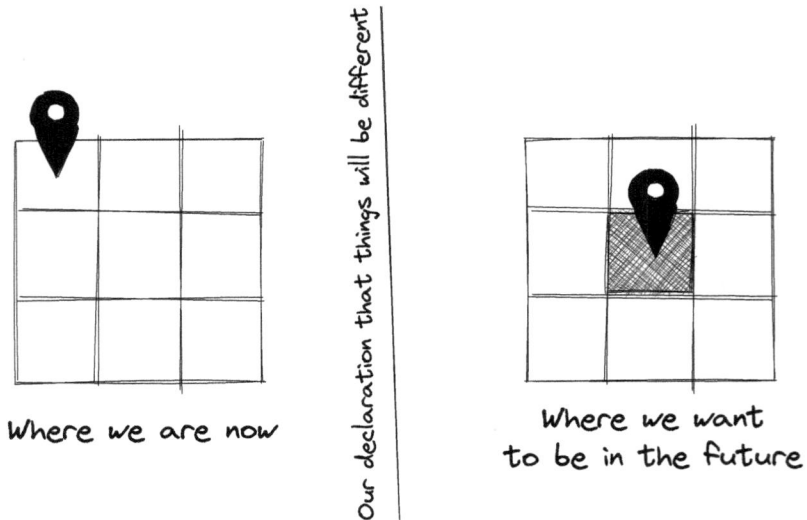

Where we are now

Our declaration that things will be different

Where we want to be in the future

Figure 14: *A declaration draws a line between where we are and where we want to be*

To declare that there is an issue, we can either make a private or public declaration. A private declaration is a declaration we make to ourselves, whereas a public declaration is a declaration we make to others. We can choose which type of declaration we would like to make for this step. Sometimes a private declaration is enough, whereas, at other times or in different situations, it might serve us better for the declaration to be public.

The key to this step is to ensure the declaration is stated aloud as a declaration, even if you are declaring it privately to yourself. It is not enough to have a fleeting thought in the back of your mind that you would like things to change. The aim of this step is to commit to changing direction. Some useful steps for doing this are:

- Pause.
- Acknowledge you want things to be different.
- Declare out loud that there is a need for change (and you want to change).
- Acknowledge you have made the declaration.
- Commit to enacting the declaration.

As with any change, declaring that there is an issue can be easier said than done. This is where it helps to ask yourself the two key questions in the model relating to your Way of Being:

1. What, in my current Way of Being, is limiting my ability to take the step of declaring that there is an issue?
2. What new Way of Being will help me take the step of declaring that there is an issue?

To support you in this step, look at what Way of Being will help you make and enact your declaration. This means understanding how your current Way of Being is serving you in taking this step and learning how to shift it to make this step a reality. To figure out exactly where shifts are required, it is beneficial to break down your Way of Being to understand what is happening in your language, moods and emotions, and body. Let's take a closer look at this process to learn what to look for.

Language

When exploring language, we want to understand the stories, opinions and interpretations that are preventing us from making the declaration and the language that will help us go ahead and declare that there is an issue. Ask yourself:

- What am I telling myself about my current situation?
- Why do I want the situation to change?
- What am I telling myself about declaring that there is an issue?
- What am I telling myself about how my situation will be after making the declaration?
- What would it take for me to shift my language (stories, opinions and interpretations) and declare that there is an issue and I want things to change?

Moods and emotions

Moods and emotions are always with us. When we notice and pay attention to our moods and emotions, we can understand how to use them to declare that we want things to change. Ask yourself:

- What moods and emotions have I attached to the situation I want to change?
- What moods and emotions are preventing me from declaring that there is an issue?
- What moods and emotions will help me declare that there is an issue and that I want things to be different?

Body

Our body is home to everything we do. However, we often overlook its role in helping us achieve outcomes. How we are in our body can significantly influence what we see as possible. Therefore, it is useful to understand what is happening in our body when attempting to declare that there is an issue. Ask yourself:

- How does my body feel when I attempt to declare that there is an issue?
- How can I shift my body so I can declare that there is an issue (and commit to enacting the declaration)?

Step 2: Seek to understand the issue

When Maggie first noticed she wanted her situation to change, all she knew was that she didn't feel as though her job was a good fit for her. While this may be a high-level explanation of what was happening, it doesn't explain what was underpinning the situation.

In Step 2, we want to become clear about what the underlying issue might be. Yes, a situation might challenge you, but what is underpinning this challenge? The goal is to seek to understand how you are viewing the situation. How are you interpreting the situation and your and others' roles in that situation? Why can't you see a different way forward? Delve down into the situation to understand why it is challenging and what within your Way of Being is leading you to take the actions you are taking.

Working through this step also sheds light on how you want the situation to be different. You can seek to understand the issue better by asking yourself a series of questions. This step is an opportunity to channel your inner three-year-old as you repeatedly dig deeper and ask yourself, 'but why?' and 'but how', and 'but what does that mean?'.

It is important to set your judgements aside in Step 2. Focus on becoming a learner so you can become clear about what you are being challenged by and what Way of Being you are operating from. You can do this by asking yourself the questions underpinning the six-step model:

1. What, in my current Way of Being, is limiting me from taking the step of becoming a learner and seeking to understand the issue?
2. What new Way of Being will help me take the step of becoming a learner and seeking to understand the issue?

Language

Asking questions helps us gain clarity. In terms of the language component of our Way of Being, the following questions can be helpful:

- What will I tell myself that will give me permission to be a learner and ask questions in this situation?
- What learning foes are present for me? How can I shift those learning foes so I can become a learner about my current situation? We discussed learning foes at length in Chapter 3, so refer back to that chapter if you would like a recap.

Moods and emotions

Our moods and emotions help us become learners about the situation and our Way of Being. The goal here is to engage your moods and emotions to support you in finding out more about how you are interpreting the situation. Curiosity and wonder can serve you in this step. Other emotions may also be useful. Ask yourself:

- What moods and emotions will help me learn more about my current situation and Way of Being?
- What moods and emotions will help me find out more about how I would like this situation to be different in the future?
- What moods and emotions would support me in shifting my Way of Being so I can change this situation in the future?

Body

When we are trying to be learners, the goal is to remain open to new ideas and possibilities. We want to create new learning to help us take the next steps forward. Focusing on the body, ask yourself:

- What am I noticing about my body now?
- What body configuration will allow me to be open to new learning?
- How will I shift to the body configuration that supports me in becoming a learner about my current situation and Way of Being?

Step 3: Explore possible ways forward

The idea in this step is to consider every possibility that presents itself as an offer you can build on. You don't need to reject possibilities immediately. In seeking possibility, you are simply looking for what you could do in the future and how you need to be to achieve the things you want to do. More specifically, what Way of Being shifts are possible to bring about new actions and outcomes?

The starting point for this step is to ask what is possible. The key is to look for possibilities that may not have been obvious to you and seek a Way of Being that will support you in doing so. You want to embrace and create possibility in this step, not shut it down. Referring again to the model, ask yourself:

1. What, in my current Way of Being, is limiting me from taking the step of seeing and creating possibility?
2. What new Way of Being will help me take the step of seeing and creating possibility?

Language

To realise what is possible, we want to use language that supports us in finding possibility. Ask yourself:

- What can I say to myself that will help me see what is possible?

Moods and emotions

Every mood and emotion creates action. The objective here is to engage moods and emotions that support you in recognising what might be possible in the future. Ask yourself:

- What moods and emotions will help me discover what future action might be possible?
- What moods and emotions will help me discover what future Way of Being might be possible?
- What moods and emotions will help me remain open to all possibilities rather than closing possibilities down?

Body

This is about looking for the body configuration that will allow you to discover what is possible. Ask yourself:

- What am I noticing about my body when I think of the situation I have declared I will change?
- How would my body be if I was to become open to seeing possibilities?
- What shifts will I make to my body configuration to support me in seeing new possibilities?

Step 4: Declare a new way forward

This step is similar to Step 1, except now you are declaring the action you will take to move the situation forward. This declaration is about being and doing. Therefore, it is important to include the new Way of Being from which you plan to take action (the doing).

As per Step 1, this declaration can be made privately or publicly. Since you are preparing to take action, it is essential not only that you make the declaration but also that you give yourself the authority to enact the declaration.

The questions to ask yourself during this step essentially mirror those in Step 1:

1. What, in my current Way of Being, is limiting my ability to take the step of declaring a new way forward?
2. What new Way of Being will help me take the step of declaring a new way forward?

Language

For this step, consider what language will support you in making a declaration you can commit to, including how you will give yourself authority to enact the declaration. Ask yourself:

- What language will support me in declaring my new way forward?

- What can I say to myself that will support me in giving authority to this declaration?
- What can I say to myself that will support me in seeing this declaration as a commitment to myself?

Moods and emotions

Here, you are looking for moods and emotions that will support you in choosing and declaring a new way forward and committing to making the new way forward a reality. Ask yourself:

- What moods and emotions will help me choose and declare my new way forward?
- What moods and emotions will help me hold this declaration as a commitment to myself?
- What moods and emotions will allow me to give myself the authority to enact the declaration?

Body

In this step, you are looking for the body configuration that will support you in taking a stand on your new way forward and preparing to take action. Ask yourself:

- What body configuration will support me in making this declaration?

Step 5: Take action

Now it's time to apply the learning you have discovered in the previous steps to your Way of Being to generate the action you have declared you will take. Since your Way of Being underpins your action, the first part of this step involves shifting your Way of Being to the Way of Being you have determined will be useful for taking action. Then, it is a matter of taking action from this Way of Being. Start by asking yourself:

1. What, in my current Way of Being, is limiting my ability to take the step of shifting my Way of Being to take action?
2. What new Way of Being will help me take the step of shifting my Way of Being to take action?

Language

For this step, consider what language will support you in shifting your Way of Being and taking action. Ask yourself:

- What can I say to myself that will support me in shifting my Way of Being and taking action?
- What can I say to myself that will support me in remaining committed to taking action?

Body

In this step, identify the body configuration that will support you in shifting your Way of Being and taking action. Ask yourself:

- What body configuration will support me in making this declaration?

Step 6: Reflect on the results

A process of reflection helps us understand what did and did not serve us in our actions. In this step, you are looking to develop habits that will support you in continuing to take action from a place of resourcefulness, making choices based on whatever served you.

As you reflect on the results you have achieved, you can seek to change your Way of Being and actions where it would serve you to do so. This enables you to start the process again at Step 1 to continue to create habits that serve you better.

This step is a little like Step 2, where you sought to gain clarity around what wasn't working. The primary difference in Step 6 is that you are now seeking to understand both what did and did not serve you in your actions. This understanding will enable you to determine whether you would like to declare further change if you believe that would be beneficial. The two questions central to the entire model also apply to this step:

1. What, in my current Way of Being, is limiting my ability to take the step of reflecting on my actions and subsequent results?

2. What new Way of Being will help me take the step of reflecting on my actions and subsequent results?

Moods and emotions

Here, you are looking for the moods and emotions that will support you in shifting your Way of Being to take action. Ask yourself:

- What moods and emotions will help me shift my Way of Being and take action?
- What moods and emotions will help me remain committed to taking this action?

Language

- What can I say to myself to support me in reflecting on my actions and results?
- What questions might help me understand whether my Way of Being, actions and results have served me?

Moods and emotions

- What moods and emotions will help me in reflecting on my Way of Being, actions and results?

Body

- What body configuration will support me in reflecting on my Way of Being, actions and results?

A last word on the six-step model for navigating life

It would be easy to fall into the trap of believing this model is about 'fixing' ourselves or righting actions we may judge as wrong. The model is about neither. Our actions are not wrong. They are legitimate for who we are being at any given point in time.

We navigate life using our prior knowledge as a tool for making decisions and taking action. For much of our life, these old ways of being and doing are useful for us. Sometimes, however, we arrive at a point where how we are being and what we are doing are not serving us.

The six-step model outlined in this chapter helps us understand and explore the ways of being and actions that will serve us as we interact with others. It is a model that supports us in *choosing* our actions rather than operating on autopilot based on our prior learning. The model is not about judging ourselves as right or wrong. It provides new ways of seeing the world so we can make effective choices regarding how we take action.

What if life came with a user guide?

In our quest to live the life we want and achieve our desired outcomes, we often focus on looking for answers. Our need for answers comes from not knowing. More specifically, we don't know how to navigate the challenge before us, so we respond by seeking answers. But how do we find the answer when we don't understand the question?

This book is an invitation to live in questions. Now that we are coming to the end of it, I invite you to look for the questions you wouldn't usually see. This invitation is not to answer the questions immediately but to sit with them, ask more questions and use them to help create new choices for responding to everyday life events and circumstances.

The core idea in this book is that, in every given moment, each of us operates from a Way of Being. That means our Way of Being is the source of the action we take. If you can understand your current and preferred ways of being, you can appreciate how your actions are being manifested and what is helping and limiting you. Our Way of Being is also a source of great learning. Understand how you are being, and you will understand what you are doing and why.

How to access your Way of Being as a source of learning

When we set aside our self-judgements and become curious about our Way of Being, we can tap into a well of information about how we are seeing the world and why. This new information offers new perspectives, allowing us to reframe our experience and take more effective action. We seek this new information by asking questions of ourselves. So, what questions should we ask?

Ask the questions you wouldn't normally think to ask. Be curious. Become a learner. It is useful to start with some overarching questions to live by in any given situation, such as:

- Why am I thinking, feeling, saying or sensing what I am?
- What is it within my Way of Being that is leading me to interpret the world the way I do?
- How am I using my language, moods and emotions, and body to create these interpretations?

The meaning we create through life and the learning we take from that meaning are embedded in our Way of Being, making our Way of Being key to every action we take. When the questions you create for yourself allow you to tap into your Way of Being, you are tapping into the closest thing any of us has to a user guide.

Does that mean life *does* come with a user guide? Well, figuratively speaking, yes, it does. But it is not a user guide with all the answers because we can't know the answers without knowing the questions. Rather, we access our user guide when we become curious enough to ask ourselves questions about how we are being in life. So, this book is an invitation for you to access your own inbuilt user guide. I encourage you to:

1. Use the six-step model outlined in this chapter to develop a practice of reflection that supports you in gaining access to insights about your Way of Being.

2. Use the ideas provided to find the questions you weren't previously able to see and apply your new learning in whatever way is relevant to you and your circumstances.

If nothing else comes from your reading of this book, I hope you have gained the ability to look for the questions you don't normally seek. When you can do this, you will have access to your own user guide for navigating everyday life.

Some final thoughts about emotions

As humans, we don't always use our emotions to support us in taking action. We label emotions as good, bad, right or wrong. We judge them and hold unhealthy views about what we should or shouldn't feel. We believe displaying emotions makes us 'emotional'. Overall, our approach to emotions is not always helpful.

My life reached a turning point when I came to see emotions as a source of data that shows us how we view the world. Emotions give us cues and help us make choices. They are always with us, moving us into action based on how we see and respond to the world. This raises the question: *If people feel how they feel for a reason, why don't we help them navigate their emotions rather than judging them or implying that their feelings are wrong?* Our view of emotions is something I hope to help change in the world.

My first introduction to emotions as a source of learning came from Alan Sieler. Later, I discovered the work of Dan Newby and his separate collaborations with Lucy Núñez and Curtis Watkins. Their collective insights opened my eyes to the power that can come from seeing emotions as signs. My world shifted in ways I never thought possible. I am grateful for this awakening and actively share these insights in my work with others.

Throughout this book, I use interpretations of emotions that derive from the works of Newby and Núñez, and Newby and Watkins. The story, inclination for action and purpose of the emotions I discuss in this book came from their work. However, the way I have applied their interpretations is my own work. I have used ideas from their books and from Newby's courses and have tried to apply this learning to help others who are navigating the challenges of everyday life. I appreciate Dan Newby very generously giving his time to review my interpretations of his work for this book and for offering tweaks and suggestions as appropriate.

I hope this book has introduced you, the reader, to a new way of looking at emotions, to see them for what they truly are – messengers doing their job, not as right, wrong, good, bad, positive or negative. Switching to this perspective has been an enormous gift for me, and it is a gift I believe others should receive too.

Free gift for readers

As a mark of my gratitude and appreciation for buying and reading my book, I invite you to download your free reader gift:

https://leadingandbeing.com/FreeReaderGift

About the author

Deanne Duncombe is a qualified ontological coach and facilitator who helps everyday people find their peace with the daily challenges of life. She has written several blogs and articles that employ ontological ideas, particularly in emotional literacy. These narratives are available on her various blog sites: anontologicallife. com and leadingandbeing.com.

Deanne is the owner of Leading and Being, a coaching and facilitation business aimed at helping people find effective ways of dealing with the challenges they may face in everyday life. She also develops programs and workshops where she shares and expands on the ideas in this book. All her programs are grounded in ontology.

Deanne lives in Canberra, Australia, with her husband, their two daughters, two rabbits and two cats. *What if Life Came With a User Guide? How to overcome negative self-talk, deal with difficult people and adjust to challenging situations* is Deanne's first book.

If you would like to contact Deanne in relation to this book or the programs she offers through Leading and Being, please email deanne@leadingandbeing.com or visit leadingandbeing.com.

References

'A manager's guide to difficult conversations in the workplace'. (Accessed 4 June, 2023). *Fair Work Australia*. https://www. fairwork.gov.au/sites/default/files/migration/712/managers-guide-to-difficult-conversations-in-the-workplace.pdf

'Authority'. (Accessed April 16, 2022). In *Cambridge Online*. https://dictionary.cambridge.org/dictionary/english/authority

Baker, W. E. (2020). *All you have to do is ask: How to master the most important skill for success* (First Edition). Currency.

Blake, A. (2018). *Your Body is Your Brain: Leverage your somatic intelligence to find purpose, build resilience, deepen relationships and lead more powerfully.* Trokay Press.

Boyer, L. (2011). *Connect: Affective leadership for effective results.* Leadership Options.

Brenner, G. F. (2018). *Suffering is optional: A spiritual guide to freedom from self-judgment & feelings of inadequacy.* New Harbinger Publications, Inc.

Brothers, C. (2005). *Language and the Pursuit of Happiness.* New Possibilities Press.

Cunningham, L. (2016). *Taking conversations from difficult to doable: 3 models to master tough conversations.* Fire Starter Publishing.

Damasio, A. (2006). *Descartes' Error: Emotion, Reason and the Human Brain.*

Daywalt, D. (2013). *The day the crayons quit.* (O. Jeffers, Illus.). HarperCollins Children's Books.

'Declaration'. (Accessed April 9, 2022). In *Cambridge Online*. https://dictionary.cambridge.org/dictionary/english/declaration

Dickins, M. (2020). *Improvise!: Use the secrets of improv to achieve extraordinary results at work.* Icon Books Ltd.

'Difficult'. (Accessed May 31, 2022). In *Cambridge Online.* https://dictionary.cambridge.org/dictionary/english/difficult

Flores, F. (2012). *Conversations For Action and Collected Essays: Instilling A Culture of Commitment in Our Working Relationships.* USA, CreateSpace Independent Publishing Platform

Flores, G. P. (2016). *Learning to learn and the navigation of moods: The meta-skill for the acquisition of skills.* Pluralistic Networks Publishing.

Fogel, A. (2021). *Restorative embodiment and resilience: A guide to disrupt habits, create inner peace, deepen relationships, and feel greater presence.* North Atlantic Books.

Gazipura, A. (2019). *On My Own Side: Transform self-criticism and doubt into permanent self-worth and confidence.* B.C. Allen Publishing and Tonic.

Goleman, D. (1996). *Emotional intelligence: Why it can matter more than IQ.* Bloomsbury Publishing Plc.

Hamill, P. (2013). *Embodied leadership: The somatic approach to developing your leadership.* Kogan Page Limited.

Harris, R. (2007). *The Happiness Trap: Stop struggling, start living.* Exisle Publishing.

Heidegger, M. (2004). *What Is Called Thinking?* trans. J. G. Gray. New York. Perennial. (Original work published 1951-1952. Original translation published 1976).

Holloway, R. (2020). *Stories we tell ourselves: Making meaning in a meaningless universe.* Canongate Books.

Kegan, R. (1998). *In over our heads: The mental demands of modern life.* Cambridge, Mass. Harvard University Press.

Kegan, R., & Lahey, L. L. (2001). *How the way we talk can change the way we work: Seven languages for transformation.* Jossey-Bass.

Lynn, E. (2020). *Dancing with Change: Cultivating healthy organisations.* cultureQs.

Newby, D., & Núñez, L. (2017). *The Unopened Gift: A primer in emotional literacy.* Daniel Newby.

Newby, D., & Watkins, C. (2019). *The Field Guide to Emotions: A Practical Orientation to 150 Essential Emotions.* Daniel Newby.

Olalla, J. (2004). From Knowledge to Wisdom: *Essays on the Crisis in Contemporary Learning.* Newfield Network, Inc.

Parkyn, C. (2009). *Human design: Discover the person you were born to be: introducing a revolutionary system that unlocks your true potential.* London, Harper Collins Publishers.

Sharma, R. (2020). *What Will People Think?: How to be Confident in Yourself and Stop Worrying about What People Think (Boost Your Self-Esteem and Confidence Book 1).* Roma Sharma.

Sieler, A. (2003). *Coaching to the Human Soul: Ontological Coaching and Deep Change: Vol. I.* Newfield Institute.

Sieler, A. (2007). *Coaching to the Human Soul: Ontological Coaching and Deep Change: Vol. II.* Newfield Institute

Sieler, A. (2012). *Coaching to the Human Soul: Ontological Coaching and Deep Change: Vol. III.* Newfield Institute

Singer, M. A. (2007). *The Untethered Soul: The journey beyond yourself.* New Harbinger Publications.

Singh, K. D. (2017). *Unbinding: The grace beyond self.* Wisdom.

Solomon, R. C., & Flores, F. (2001). *Building trust in business, politics, relationships, and life.* Oxford University Press.

Steiner, C. M. (2003). *Emotional literacy intelligence with a heart.* Personhood Press.

Tyrrell, M. (2014). *New ways of seeing: The art of therapeutic reframing: how to use your words to release your clients from limiting beliefs, including examples from 81 real cases.* Uncommon Knowledge.

Index

Singer, Michael A 8

Singh, Kathleen Dowling 9

six-step model for navigating life xx-vii, 64, 199, 200, 201, 211, 212, 214

  step 1 65, 200, 202, 203, 204

  step 2 65, 200, 202, 205, 206

  step 3 65, 200, 207, 208

  step 4 65, 200, 208, 209

  step 5 65, 200, 209, 210, 211

  step 6 65, 200, 210, 211

  two key questions 201, 203, 205, 207, 208, 209, 210

Solomon, Robert C 104, 191

speaking up 162, 165, 166, 167, 168, 169, 170, 171, 175, 176, 177, 181

standards for living life 31, 58

Steiner, Claude 133

stories, our xxiv, 8, 9, 13, 15, 19, 31, 32, 33, 42, 43, 45, 53, 61, 62, 63, 78, 81, 83, 84, 85, 102, 103, 106, 110, 111, 112, 121, 125, 149, 150, 153, 163, 166, 167, 169, 171, 203, 204

suffering, our personal xxvi, 3, 8, 9, 11, 20, 30, 83, 119, 122

T

trust 13, 94, 95, 96, 99, 100, 103, 104, 105, 106, 113, 118, 120, 164, 170, 185, 186, 191, 192

  choosing how we trust ourselves 105

  shifting our level of self-trust 105

  trusting ourselves 105

trust, space of 191, 192, 195

trust, the four judgements of 104, 105, 186

  competence 94, 96, 104, 105, 186

  engagement 104, 105, 186

  reliability 104, 105, 186

  sincerity 104, 105, 186

truth, living our stories as the 8, 128, 143, 145, 149, 150, 161, 188, 193, 199

Tyrrell, Mark 153, 154

U

uncertainty 16, 47, 73, 74, 75, 76, 77, 78, 79, 80, 81, 83, 85, 86, 87, 88, 97, 106, 110, 111, 112, 119, 188

W

Watkins, Curtis 101, 105, 106, 107, 108, 215

Way of Being xxiv, xxv, xxvi, xxvii, xxviii, 18, 40, 42, 43, 44, 45, 46, 53, 54, 55, 56, 58, 59, 60, 61, 63, 64, 65, 66, 73, 82, 83, 84, 85, 89, 90, 93, 102, 103, 104, 106, 112, 120, 121, 123, 124, 127, 132, 135, 143, 144, 145, 148, 152, 153, 154, 155, 156, 157, 165, 166, 167, 169, 171, 172, 173, 175, 176, 183, 184, 185, 186, 189, 190, 191, 192, 193, 194, 195, 199, 200, 201, 203, 205, 206, 207, 208, 209, 210, 211, 213, 214

wonder 16, 22, 80, 81, 82, 88, 135, 167, 206

worry. *See* worrying

worrying 31, 33, 55, 62, 70, 74, 75, 76, 77, 94, 111, 124, 162

worrying about what other people will think 164, 167, 172, 173, 175

worthiness 155, 171, 173, 174

www.ingramcontent.com/pod-product-compliance
Lightning Source LLC
Chambersburg PA
CBHW072102020426
42334CB00017B/1599